MICHELANNE FORSTER

DAUGHTERS OF HEAVEN

New Zealand Playscripts

GENERAL EDITOR: JOHN THOMSON

Glide Time by Roger Hall
Middle Age Spread by Roger Hall
Awatea by Bruce Mason
The Pohutukawa Tree by Bruce Mason
The Two Tigers by Brian McNeill
State of the Play by Roger Hall
Jack Winter's Dream by James K Baxter
Foreskin's Lament by Greg McGee
Bruce Mason Solo (hardcover)
Blood of the Lamb by Bruce Mason
Fifty-Fifty by Roger Hall
Hot Water by Roger Hall
Outside In by Hilary Beaton
The End of the Golden Weather by Bruce Mason
Out in the Cold by Greg McGee
Tooth and Claw by Greg McGee
Shuriken by Vincent O'Sullivan
Objection Overruled by Carolyn Burns
Wednesday to Come by Renée
Driftwood by Rachel McAlpine
Pass It On by Renée
Coaltown Blues by Mervyn Thompson
The Healing Arch by Bruce Mason
Squatter by Stuart Hoar
The Share Club by Roger Hall
A Red Mole Sketchbook by Alan Brunton
Three Radio Plays
Jones & Jones by Vincent O'Sullivan
The Land of the Moa by George Leitch
Billy by Vincent O'Sullivan
Jeannie Once by Renée
Broken Arse by Bruce Stewart
Daughters of Heaven by Michelanne Forster

IN PREPARATION:

Joyful and Triumphant by Robert Lord
Lovelock's Dream Run by David Geary

DAUGHTERS OF HEAVEN

Michelanne Forster

Victoria University Press

VICTORIA UNIVERSITY PRESS
Victoria University of Wellington
PO Box 600 Wellington

© Michelanne Forster 1992

ISBN 0 86473 240 6

First published 1992, reprinted 1997

Permission to perform this play must be obtained from PLAYMARKET,
PO Box 9767, Courtenay Place, Wellington, New Zealand.
The publishers acknowledge the assistance and advice
of PLAYMARKET, which was established in 1973 to
provide services for New Zealand playwrights.

Published with the assistance of
a grant from the Literature Programme of the
Queen Elizabeth II Arts Council
of New Zealand

This book is copyright. Apart from
any fair dealing for the purpose of private study,
research, criticism or review, as permitted under the
Copyright Act, no part may be reproduced by any
process without the permission of
the publishers

Printed GP Print, Wellington

To Paul

First Performance

Daughters of Heaven was first performed at the Court Theatre, Christchurch, on 19 October 1991 with the following cast:

Juliet Hulme	Nancy Schröder
Pauline Parker	Louise Frost
Bridget O'Malley	Yvonne Martin
Hilda Hulme	Darien Takle
Henry Hulme/ Justice Adams	Patrick Dowman
Walter Perry/ Reg Medlicott	Ross Gumbley
Alan Brown/Detective	Mark Hadlow
Honora Rieper/Matron	Sandra Rasmussen
Herbert Rieper/ Terrence Gresson	Paul Barrett

Directed by Elric Hooper
Designed by Tony Geddes

Foreword

Few people alive and residing in Christchurch in 1954 have difficulty in remembering the circumstances of hearing the news that a woman called Rieper had been murdered in Victoria Park, or recalling the guilty excitement as the details, not just of the crime but of the private lives of those connected with the perpetrators, were revealed.

I was a first year student at Canterbury College at the time. I remember leaning against a green corrugated iron fence, balancing my bike, and exchanging wonder with someone equally ill-informed about life. I heard the word 'lesbian' for the first time. Then, one day soon after, through a stack in the university library, I heard a distinguished historian, an eminent lecturer on Arab civilisation, deliver himself of a stream of malicious detail about the case. I was shocked, not so much at what I heard, as at who had said it. I thought only the uneducated like myself spoke like that.

I suppose, as with so many others, the Parker-Hulme case was part of my education, loss of provincial innocence and the beginning of disillusion.

So when Michelanne Forster approached me about writing a play for the Court Theatre on the subject, I was enthusiastic—it was part of my life, part of the lore of this city and, most important, an engrossing and bizarre story.

I also felt enough time had gone by—nearly forty years—for the events to have become history—history meaning the record of the past that can be contemplated in a detached and critical manner. In this last assumption, I could not have been more wrong. The moment word got about that we were going to re-open the case, albeit in theatrical—or perhaps, especially in theatrical—terms, the air was full of the sound of rising hackles and phrases like 'bad taste'. Some people refused to talk about the case, while others would not stop. It was as if the story was still the personal and private possession of even those who had only the slightest contact with the events. The Parker-Hulme case was still a touchy subject.

Michelanne Forster found two main sources for the play: the public record of the trial as it exists in the almost verbatim reports that appeared in the two major daily papers of the city, and interviews with survivors. Several people refused to speak to her, and several more were very guarded. However, through polite and persistent enquiry, she was able to assemble facts and, more important for the theatre, idiosyncratic detail that brought both the personalities and the provincial atmosphere of Christchurch in 1954 to life.

Michelanne Forster's play operates on at least three levels.

The external and legal facts are established by the prosecuting council, Alan Brown. This provides the simple narrative.

At the same time a commentary on the events is carried on by another outside observer, Bridget. This is not so much a fictional creation as a being in whom are gathered together opinions, attitudes and facts manifested in the city at the time. The case brought out all the small-town prejudices one would expect to find in a place like Christchurch in 1954: anti-intellectualism, hypocritical disapproval of sexual misconduct, religious bigotry, and strange survivals of folk superstitions such as those surrounding tuberculosis.

Between these two poles, the events of the case are recreated in a series of more-or-less naturalistic scenes—though these scenes are not always presented in strictly chronological order.

Perhaps where these three lines intersect, tragic understanding may occur.

While strictly adhering to the facts of the case and yet liberating observers from the need to say, 'It didn't happen like that', the play is presented in a manner that distances the events—but not so much that they become unreal. This is, indeed, making a virtue of necessity for no theatre can accurately present each locale in such a complex story.

Ultimately the aim of any play, whether based on fact or presented as total fiction, is to present a world, no matter how

Foreword

strange or extreme, which is consistent within itself and convinces solely by itself.

When it was pointed out to Michelangelo that his statue of Lorenzo de' Medici looked nothing like the real man, the great artist replied that in a hundred years no one would know that, but everyone would be convinced that this marble image was how such a noble person ought to have looked. Such is the aspiration, arrogance and sometimes the magical metamorphosis of art.

Elric Hooper
Artistic Director
Court Theatre

Introduction

When I first heard the story of the Parker Hulme murder I was both repelled and fascinated. I had just given birth to my son Mathias and as I cradled my tiny helpless babe I could scarcely bear to think about Mrs Parker lying on a track in Victoria Park, her head bashed in by a half brick in a stocking. A mother's brutal death by the hand of her own child seemed then, and now, the most grotesque of crimes to me. Once, late at night, I felt the presence of Mrs Parker so strongly I was afraid if I turned around I would see her face to face in the corner of my study. But gradually, as I immersed myself in the project, I became dulled, much the same way the slaughterman does as he slits the throat of a beast. The 'moider' became just another scene on a page.

Many Cantabrians remembered the murder and most people I approached were willing to talk to me. I was surprised, in fact, by the intensity of their recollections: information was never given lightly—the story still had the power to wound. Women tended to voice the same bewildered sentiment. *How could this have happened—here in Christchurch?* Men were, on the whole, much more reticent. They didn't like speculating. *It was a long time ago; I don't recall. The girls were punished and what's to be gained from talking about it now?* I collected a notebook of fragmented memories and it was these small stories which launched me towards the larger story I was after. I was hunting the psychological heart of the murder.

The play went through a number of rewrites. In the first draft the play seemed to be about the nature of insanity. In the next draft it seemed to be about being undone by love. The character of Bridget gradually grew stronger with each draft as her preoccupation with trying to find a meaning for an inexplicable act began to be mine as well. 'Evil' poked its ugly head into the proceedings and added to the babble as well. With each draft I had more and more difficulty keeping the play 'tidy'. The characters began taking on a life of their own and pushed their way out of the page to deliver ultimatums to me. They all wanted their own viewpoints presented and they all wanted equal time. I was most relieved to be assured by Elric Hooper, the Artistic Director of the Court Theatre, who had commissioned the play, that in his view the strength of the piece lay in these many layers of conflicting viewpoint. He encouraged me not to iron out or flatten contradictions and differing points of view but rather to nourish them and allow the play to take on a texture created by complexity.

When people ask me now, 'What is the play about?' I find it nearly impossible to answer. Like a crystal, it has many sides to it which all contribute to making the whole. Look one way and it's the story of a provincial New Zealand city being turned upside down by a murder. It's the story of Christchurch in 1954, restrained and *nice* with implicit British attitudes about class and gender suddenly being confronted with evil. On the outskirts of the city's level lawns and daffodil gardens two girls picnic with the devil.

Look another way and *Daughters of Heaven* is about love—that powerful emotion which sweeps reason and morality away in a crazy tide of two-ness. 'We had the right to do what we needed to in the interests of our own happiness,' says Juliet Hulme. The question of the girls' lesbianism (which seems to preoccupy the media) never worried me. It was the passionate delivery of their souls to one another that I was concerned with—not what they did in bed.

People inevitably ask me, 'Where are Juliet and Pauline now?' I can truthfully reply I don't know the answer. While researching the play I shied away from looking for Parker and Hulme. The murder and society's subsequent punishment belong to history—for murder, however privately conceived, is a public act. But once the girls were released from prison I believe our 'right' to their story ends. Their lives are now their own.

When I finally finished writing *Daughters of Heaven* I was eager to be the play's mouthpiece. I sat in the rehearsal room at the Court Theatre ready to interpret and explain all my intentions to the cast. I soon discovered that the play spoke for itself, thank you very much, and didn't require me any longer. Each director, designer and actor who has worked on *Daughters of Heaven* has added life to the text and exploded the play's original boundaries. It has been a privilege to witness the ongoing life of the play separate from myself. I've learned there's always a time for letting go and, when it comes, it's really rather restful.

Michelanne Forster
November 1992

Acknowledgements

I would like to thank Elric Hooper, Artistic Director of the Court Theatre, whose vision of the play's potential sustained and encouraged me throughout its creation. I would also like to thank the citizens of Christchurch who chose to share their memories with me, the Court Theatre Company, Colin McColl, Geraldine Brophy and Lisa Warrington.

Author's Note

Courtroom testimony and Pauline's diary quotations are taken from court reports as recorded in the Christchurch *Press* and the Christchurch *Star Sun*. All other dialogue is fictional.

Characters

JULIET HULME. Daughter of Henry and Hilda Hulme. Fifteen and a half.
PAULINE PARKER. Daughter of Honora Parker and Herbert Rieper. Sixteen.
BRIDGET O'MALLEY. The Hulmes' maid. Irish.
HILDA HULME. Juliet's mother. British.
DR HENRY HULME. Juliet's father. British.
HONORA MARY RIEPER. Pauline's mother. Forty-five.
HERBERT RIEPER. Pauline's father. Sixty.
ALAN BROWN. Crown Prosecutor.
TERRENCE GRESSON. Counsel for Juliet Hulme.
WALTER PERRY. Hilda Hulme's lover.
DR REGINALD MEDLICOTT. Psychiatrist for the Defence.
JUSTICE ADAMS
POLICE DETECTIVE
POLICE MATRON
PRISON OFFICER

This play can be performed by nine actors with the following doubling:

WALTER PERRY/REGINALD MEDLICOTT
HENRY HULME/JUSTICE ADAMS/PRISON OFFICER
HERBERT RIEPER/TERRENCE GRESSON
ALAN BROWN/POLICE DETECTIVE
HONORA RIEPER/POLICE MATRON

> The weak will never enter the kingdom of love
> for it is a harsh ungenerous kingdom . . .
>
> Gabriel García Márquez
> *Love in the Time of Cholera*

> First of all, I wept to God
> —when the world is wet & shy, under
> the bridge I hold her
> head down under
> water & I feel her thrash
> against me, just this once, I murder
> her,
> it's a once in a lifetime thing you
> know?
> You have no idea
> how much I love her, I am she.
>
> Lucy Brock Broido

Act One

★ Scene One

New Zealand, 1959. The action is divided between PAULINE's *prison cell in Christchurch and* JULIET's *prison cell in Wellington, where the girls have been transferred in preparation for their release. They have been in prison, separately, since October 1954.*

PAULINE: O my God, I am heartily sorry—
JULIET: My dear one. I am dictating this to you through the spirits of the Fourth World, per usual.
PAULINE: —I am heartily sorry for having offended thee and I detest sin above every other evil because it offends thee my God who art worthy of all my love—
JULIET: I want you to remember Paradise. It was ours once. We created our own map of Heaven. Haven't I learned the hard way in this shit-hole of a place that that is all there is? Our Heaven and the two of us?
PAULINE: —and I firmly resolve, by thy holy Grace, never more to offend thee and to amend my life.
JULIET: Now that I have been brought to my knees I see my own star brighter than ever. I will never give in. I will never look back. I will never regret. It is our fate.
PAULINE: Amen.

Scene Two

BRIDGET, *addressing the audience*: The 'domestic tragedy' was how Mrs Hulme referred to it after. That and 'Juliet's illness', as if wickedness was something you caught from breathing bad air. But I didn't blame her. Not much. In the beginning we were pals.

The Hulmes' house.

HILDA *enters.*

HILDA: I do hope you'll be happy here.
BRIDGET: It looks a very nice situation.
HILDA: You like the flat?
BRIDGET: It's lovely, thank you.
HILDA: Feel free to borrow anything from our kitchen until you get settled—plates, cups, saucepans—
BRIDGET: You're too kind, Mrs Hulme, really.
HILDA: No, Hilda. Please. You must call me Hilda. We don't stand on ceremony in this house.
BRIDGET: In that case please call me Bridget.
HILDA: Lovely. Bridget.
BRIDGET: Thank you, Hilda.
HILDA: I'll leave it to you then. Bridget.
BRIDGET: Right. Hilda.

HILDA *goes out.*

Bridget, Hilda. Hilda, Bridget. We sounded like a couple of chooks at the back gate. Her husband Henry was Cambridge educated. Couldn't understand a word he said.

HENRY *enters.*

HENRY: Mrs O'Malley. It appears I shall be unavoidably incarcerated in the Ivory Tower past dinner time. Would you mind terribly keeping whatever delectable morsel you conjure up warm for me until I return? *He leaves.*
BRIDGET: Still, he was a gentleman. Not like some of those other university types buggering each other behind closed doors calling it research. He wasn't like that. Hilda was the one you had to watch out for. I soon discovered that. She talked equal but she acted like a Queen Bee—until her daughter was arrested for murder.

The courtroom.

BROWN, *the Crown Prosecutor, is addressing the jury.*

BROWN: Most of you will have read in the newspapers, and no doubt have discussed among your friends, the story of the crime. One of my duties is to ask you to endeavour to forget all you have read or heard about the case, and indeed it is your duty to do so. You are here to decide the case on the evidence and on the evidence alone.

You may pity the dead woman, the mother of the girl Parker, who was brutally done to death, or you may feel pity for the accused in the dreadful situation they find themselves in today. These things have nothing to do with this trial at all. Sentiment and emotionalism have no part in British justice.

BRIDGET: British justice. Hah! There isn't a person in this courtroom—or in the whole of Christchurch—who isn't salivating over every detail.

BROWN: Before hearing the evidence of the killing of Mrs Parker it is important you should know something of the accused and their families. Let us begin with the girls themselves. After meeting at Christchurch Girls' High School two years ago, their friendship developed rapidly into what may be called an intense devotion for each other.

BRIDGET: Aye, the girls were devoted, I'll give you that. Pauline was devoted to Juliet and Juliet was devoted to herself.

Scene Three

1953. JULIET's bedroom, late afternoon. Coronation music: Handel's Zadok the Priest.

PAULINE is dressed as Lancelot Trelawny, a soldier of fortune. She ritualistically lights candles then scatters dried leaves and weeds. JULIET is dressed as the Emperor Diello, evil ruler of their imaginary kingdom of Borovnia and Volumnia.

PAULINE: Fennel, dock and wandering Jew, take root. Convolvulus and periwinkle, flourish throughout the land. Prickly gorse and deadly belladonna, entwine together to pierce the hearts of our enemies. Poison, plague and pestilence, ready yourselves to strike on command of the dreaded Diello. We bow before you Diello, son of the Emperor Charles II and his Mistress Deborah.

JULIET: Rise and utter the challenge.

PAULINE, *throwing one of* HILDA's *evening gloves to the ground*: If any person of high or low degree shall deny our Sovereign Lord Diello, heir to the Imperial Crown of Borovnia and Volumnia, here is his champion who sayeth he lyeth and is a false traitor. I stand ready in person to combat in this quarrel and adventure with my life.

JULIET, *holding up a chalice*: To the health and long life of my champion! *She drinks then gives the chalice to* PAULINE. Craven masses, hear the words of the mighty Diello. He has toppled his ancient father from the throne and vows to rule according to the law of a new generation. There will be no mercy to those who disobey me. Neither to the snotty-nosed orphan or the simpering sibling; nor to the fish-fingered housewife or the hunch-backed academic. All must cower before me and obey the wisdom of the Royal Law. The lively oracles of God are mine alone.

PAULINE, *putting* HILDA's *fur stole around* JULIET's *shoulders*: The mantle of greatness descends upon you.

JULIET: Vivat Borovnia!

PAULINE, *putting a ring on* JULIET's *finger*: The Ring of Fortitude. Given to you by Lancelot Trelawny your true and faithful liege man. He will live and die in thy earthly worship.

JULIET: Vivat Volumnia!

PAULINE, *placing a crown on* JULIET's *head*: The Crown of Desire. For the weak shall never enter the Kingdom of Love.

JULIET: Vivat Diello! Anoint me.

PAULINE, *anointing* JULIET *with oil and intoning*: And as Solomon was anointed by Zadok the Priest and Nathan the Prophet be thou anointed Emperor of Borovnia and Volumnia.

> JULIET *tilts her face to be kissed on the lips.* BRIDGET O'MALLEY *calls out.*

BRIDGET: Juliet? Juliet!

JULIET: Bloody hell. Blow out the candles, quick! *She calls*: Hold on a moment!

> JULIET *throws the coronation regalia into a corner.* PAULINE *quickly dresses, blowing out candles at same time.*

BRIDGET, *coming closer*: What are you doing in there?

JULIET: Nothing.

> BRIDGET *raps on the door.* PAULINE *opens it on* JULIET's *signal.*

PAULINE: Hello, Mrs O'Malley.
BRIDGET: What in God's Holy Name is that stink? I smelled it right down in the kitchen.
PAULINE: It's incense.
BRIDGET: You've been smoking again, haven't you.
PAULINE: No, Mrs O'Malley.
BRIDGET: I smell fags underneath that stink.
PAULINE: It's candles. We were playing a game.
BRIDGET: You'll be back in the sanatorium if you don't watch out. You should be resting.
JULIET: I am resting.
BRIDGET: Wallowing's more like it. Look at this room. It's not fit for a pig. *She starts to tidy up.*
JULIET: I thought it was your day off.
BRIDGET: It's not.
JULIET: But I thought—
BRIDGET: Thought stuck a feather in the ground and thought it would grow a hen. God help us. There's muck all over the carpet. *She holds up a weed.* Well?
JULIET: It's a weed.
BRIDGET: I do have eyes.
PAULINE: We'll tidy everything up.
BRIDGET: I should say so. I don't get paid to hoover weeds. *She notices wax from the candles.* What's this? *She picks at the wax then looks at* PAULINE. Don't stand there gaping like a fish. Fetch a rag and some Tan-ol from the wash house.
JULIET: I'll come with you.
BRIDGET: You'll do no such thing.

> JULIET *reluctantly stays.* PAULINE *goes out.*

BRIDGET: I've a mind to tell your father about your pranks.
JULIET: He doesn't care.
BRIDGET: He cares about smoking in the bedroom.
JULIET: We were not smoking.
BRIDGET: O, aye.

JULIET: Do you mind, Bridget? I've got a headache.
BRIDGET: Aren't we the little actress.
JULIET: I don't feel well.
BRIDGET: I'm not surprised. Cooped up in your bedroom all day talking rubbish and scribbling it down like it was the holy writ.
JULIET: For your information, Gina and I are writing a novel.
BRIDGET: Ooh, a novel?
JULIET: Yes.
BRIDGET: And what's the novel about?
JULIET: Nothing you'd be interested in. Philosophy. Love. Higher things.
BRIDGET: Don't you go putting on airs with me. I saw you two running around the garden in your knickers last week.
JULIET: It was hot.
BRIDGET: Very hot I'm sure.
JULIET: We were sunbathing.
BRIDGET: I know mischief when I see it.
JULIET: Some people are so narrow minded.
BRIDGET: Some people had better say why they were thrashing about in the ferns shouting mumbo jumbo or I'll be forced to tell their Mam.
JULIET: We were burying religion.
BRIDGET: Holy Mother of God.
JULIET: First we sent Mario Lanza up to the Gods and then we sacrificed a mouse at the temple of Minerva. We baptised him 'Randolf'.
BRIDGET: You're making yourself an easy target for the devil. Mark my words.
JULIET: Isn't it strange about names? You've got Bridget imprinted on your forehead but there's no way on earth Pauline is a Pauline or I'm a Juliet. Our mothers made a terrible mistake. That's why we had to re-christen ourselves Deborah and Gina.
BRIDGET: In my humble opinion you're both headed straight for the fires of Hell.
JULIET: Thank you for your concern, Bridget. I'll bear that in mind.
HILDA, *off*: Juliet! *She enters, beautifully dressed.* Hello darling. I'm off.
JULIET: You look sumptuous.
HILDA: I'm meeting Daddy at the Bennetts' in half an hour.

ACT 1   23

JULIET: Will Mr Perry be there?
HILDA: Maybe.
JULIET: How divine.
HILDA: Where's Pauline?
JULIET: Bridget sent her to the wash house.
BRIDGET: The girls are set on ruining the furniture.
JULIET: We dripped one tiny bit of wax.
HILDA: You mustn't annoy Mrs O'Malley, darling. We couldn't manage without her.
JULIET: I could.
HILDA: Juliet. Don't. *She strokes* JULIET*'s brow.* You're hot.
BRIDGET: I've told her—get some fresh air, I said. Lying about all afternoon with the drapes drawn. It's like a furnace in here.
HILDA: Have you taken your medicine?
BRIDGET: If I've told her once I've told her a hundred times—
JULIET: I hate the taste. I'd rather have a cocktail.
HILDA: So would I.
PAULINE, *entering*: I'm sorry, Mrs O'Malley. I couldn't find the— oh, good afternoon, Mrs Hulme.
HILDA: Hello Pauline.
PAULINE: You look very nice.
HILDA: Thank you. That tunic suits you too.
PAULINE: It's a costume. We were doing a scene.
HILDA: Really.
JULIET: From one of our books.
BRIDGET: She was flinging dead leaves about here, there and everywhere.
JULIET: It was a symbolic action, Bridget.
BRIDGET: I'm just putting your mother in the picture.
HILDA: Using one's imagination is so important at this age. *Kissing* JULIET: Now be good darling and don't stay up too late.
JULIET: You smell so . . . delicious!
HILDA, *stopping at the door*: Oh! I almost forgot—your mother rang.
PAULINE: Yes?
HILDA: She said—could you pick up a pound of sausages on your way home. Bon soir. *She goes out.*
BRIDGET: What a pity. Pauline will miss my nice roast chicken.
JULIET: See you anon, Bridget.

BRIDGET: When Miss here gives me the Tan-ol like I asked.
PAULINE: It's gone missing. I told you.
BRIDGET: What do you mean it's gone missing? I put it in the wash house not ten minutes ago.
PAULINE: There is no Tan-ol.
BRIDGET: Don't be daft. Did you look on the shelf above the laundry tub?
PAULINE: I looked everywhere.
BRIDGET: All right then. Let the furniture fall to pieces. It's all the same to me. *She goes out.*
JULIET: Bloody busybody. Could you really not find the Tan-ol?
PAULINE: Oh, I found it. But I threw it out the wash house window.

The girls laugh gleefully.

JULIET: Well done! Gina gets her revenge.
PAULINE: If she thinks she can order me around she's got another think coming.
JULIET: Bravo! Bravissimo!
PAULINE: Your mother is so beautiful.
JULIET: She dyes her hair.
PAULINE: You look like her.
JULIET, *touching* PAULINE'*s face*: You don't look all that much like your mother. Truly.
PAULINE: I think I might be adopted.
JULIET: You're very different people inside.
PAULINE: Yes. We are.
JULIET: Oh God. I have a headache. The coronation was going so well until Bridget poked her ugly face in.
PAULINE: Diello was crowned. That's the main thing. Shall I? *She massages* JULIET'*s neck and head.*
JULIET: She was threatening me again with hellfire and damnation. She said she saw us at the temple.
PAULINE: When?
JULIET: Last week. When we sent Mario up to the gods.
PAULINE: But you can't see the temple from the house. Not even from the upstairs window.
JULIET: She must have been spying on us. Ooh, that's lovely . . . I think we should get rid of her. She's beginning to get on my nerves.

ACT I

PAULINE: As Diello commands.
JULIET: Why don't we blackmail her?
PAULINE: Yes, good.
JULIET: Mother's china ornaments, I think.

The girls assume mock-innocent voices.

PAULINE: The shepherdess? No, Mrs Hulme, I haven't seen it.
JULIET: Wasn't Mrs O'Malley the last person in the room?
PAULINE: My ring's gone missing too but I didn't want to say.
JULIET: I know it's difficult to let her go, Mother, but we can't have a thief in the house.

They burst into giggles.

PAULINE: You're disgustingly clever.
JULIET: Thank you darling. *Pause.* Mummy's giving a party on Saturday. I thought we might try getting drunk.
PAULINE: Yes.
JULIET: We'll have to do it discreetly though or Mummy will have a fit. Can you vomit into the azaleas discreetly?
PAULINE: On your command, my Lord.
JULIET: Thou good and faithful servant. Let me reward you.
PAULINE: As it pleases you, my Lord.

PAULINE kneels. JULIET undresses PAULINE. Both girls are in their underclothes. They assume the voices of film characters. JULIET is James Mason, PAULINE is Margaret Lockwood.

JULIET: My darling, don't hide your face.
PAULINE: I'm ashamed.
JULIET: Ashamed of what, my angel?
PAULINE: My past. My sordid, sordid past.
JULIET: Nothing you tell me can make any difference.
PAULINE: I'm no longer . . . pure.
JULIET, *abruptly becoming herself*: Truly? Did you finally do it with Nicholas?
PAULINE: It hurt.
JULIET: You need Vaseline. I read it in Mummy's Family Planning Manual. We'll pinch it from the chemist's . . . that can be next week's project.
PAULINE: I don't really fancy him any more.

JULIET: But you must try it again. I want you to.
PAULINE: Mario's much better.
JULIET, *becoming Mario Lanza*: Yes, of course.
PAULINE: Mario.
JULIET: Gina.
PAULINE: Mario mio.

> *They kiss.* JULIET *begins to stroke* PAULINE, *then notices her slip.*

JULIET: It's gone a bit grey and slimy hasn't it?
PAULINE: I do have a nicer one at home.
JULIET: I didn't mean—Gina, I'm sorry . . .

> PAULINE *is suddenly enraged. She rips her slip off.*

PAULINE: No, you're absolutely right. It's a filthy rag! *She tears it into shreds.*
JULIET: Pauline!
PAULINE: I hate, hate, hate wearing my sister's hand-me-downs! Everything I own has my sister's smell on it. The least Mother could do is buy me some decent underwear, stupid bitch!

> PAULINE *is trembling.* JULIET *strokes her.*

JULIET: Poor Gina.
PAULINE: She even tried to make me wear one of her old bras.
JULIET: Poor, poor Gina.

> JULIET *takes her locket off and gives it to* PAULINE.

PAULINE: Oh Deborah, I'm so happy when I'm with you.
JULIET: You're an idiot. It's only an old locket.
PAULINE: I love it. I love you.
JULIET: Don't ever leave me.
PAULINE: Never.
JULIET: Promise?
PAULINE: Promise.
JULIET: Cross your heart?
PAULINE: And hope to die.

Scene Four

The courtroom.

BROWN: The girls' main object in life was to be together, to share each other's thoughts and activities, secrets and plans. The girl Parker visited the Hulmes' residence at Ilam regularly, on occasion staying for days at a time. Mrs Parker became perturbed over their unhealthy relationship and tried to break it up. This interference was resented by the girls and gradually grew into hatred.

1953. The two girls' bedrooms. [handwritten: dining room / living room]

PAULINE *is in her underclothes writing in her diary. She is listening to* 'E lucevan le stelle' *from* Tosca.

PAULINE: Yesterday Mother was out so I went to Deborah's. No one was home so we bathed together . . . However I felt thoroughly depressed afterwards . . .

In her own bedroom [handwritten: dining room], JULIET *is writing in her diary. The music continues as both girls write, their voices overlapping.*

JULIET: We bathed for some time. Gina was very depressed. She talked about suicide. Of course her circumstances are almost intolerable.

PAULINE: Life seemed so much not worth living and death such an easy way out.

JULIET: . . . such an easy way out.

PAULINE: Anger against Mother boils up inside me. It is she who is one of the main obstacles in my path.

JULIET: . . . our path is strewn with obstacles . . .

The music swells. PAULINE *is overcome by it. She hardly hears* MRS RIEPER *knocking at the door.*

MRS RIEPER: Pauline! We're going to be late.

PAULINE *ignores her.*

You've been ~~locked up~~ [handwritten: in] there an hour and a half.

PAULINE: In a moment.

MRS RIEPER: ~~I'm opening the door right now.~~ [handwritten: I'm coming in]

PAULINE: Philistine.

> MRS RIEPER *enters with freshly ironed skirt and blouse.*

MRS RIEPER: Please turn that music off.

> PAULINE *turns it off.*

Well?

PAULINE: Well what?

MRS RIEPER: Thank you for ironing my clothes, Mother. I know I promised to do it myself but I forgot.

PAULINE: Thank you. Don't watch me!

> PAULINE *zips up her skirt.*

MRS RIEPER: That skirt's hanging on you.

PAULINE: It is not.

MRS RIEPER: You could be anaemic.

PAULINE: I feel fine.

MRS RIEPER: Your hair looks limp.

PAULINE: I like it straight.

MRS RIEPER: It was the Hulmes who recommended Dr Bennett so stop sulking.

PAULINE: Only because you went on and on.

MRS RIEPER: I did no such thing.

PAULINE: Mrs Hulme said—

MRS RIEPER: Said what?

PAULINE: Nothing.

MRS RIEPER: Don't you 'nothing' me.

PAULINE: That you're a worrier.

MRS RIEPER: She said that, did she?

PAULINE: Yes.

MRS RIEPER: If you ask me, Lady Muck should worry herself a little bit more. Don't slouch. You'll compress your innards. You really could be a lovely girl if you set your mind to it.

PAULINE: Deborah likes me the way I am.

MRS RIEPER: Why you can't call Juliet by her proper Christian name I'll never know. Deborah and Gina.

PAULINE: There's no need to harp on about it.

MRS RIEPER: You're not pining over that fellow Nicholas are you?

PAULINE, *scornfully*: Nicholas!

MRS RIEPER: I thought he was rather fond of you.
PAULINE: Maybe.
MRS RIEPER: I know you'd never do anything to disappoint me.
PAULINE: I wouldn't touch Nicholas with a barge pole.
MRS RIEPER: I wasn't suggesting—
PAULINE: If you think there was ever anything between Nicholas and me—
MRS RIEPER: Now Pauline, I've never said—
PAULINE: The thought disgusts me.
MRS RIEPER: Sometimes young people do things they regret later on.
PAULINE: Not me.
MRS RIEPER: Even your Dad's worried.
PAULINE: There's nothing wrong with me!
MRS RIEPER: Maybe you need a tonic.
PAULINE: You don't like the Hulmes, do you?
MRS RIEPER: There is such a thing as overstaying your welcome. You practically live there.
PAULINE: I'm one of the family. Mrs Hulme said so.
MRS RIEPER: I'm your mother, Pauline, not Lady Muck.
PAULINE: I'm to come out as often as I like.
MRS RIEPER: And I say no more going to Ilam until you're more cheerful around the house, and you eat properly.
PAULINE: That's not fair!
MRS RIEPER: No potatoes, no Juliet.

> BRIDGET *rings at the Riepers' front door. She has a Mario Lanza record.*

Finish getting dressed. We're leaving in five minutes. *She opens the door.* Yes?
BRIDGET: Mrs Rieper? Bridget O'Malley.
MRS RIEPER: Oh yes. Come in.
BRIDGET: Thank you. Juliet asked me to drop this record off for Pauline.
MRS RIEPER: I don't like her accepting gifts she can't repay.
BRIDGET: I think it's a loan.
MRS RIEPER: A loan. Well then.
BRIDGET: There's a note too.
MRS RIEPER: We've a doctor's appointment to keep—

BRIDGET: Nothing serious I hope.
MRS RIEPER: Pauline's not looking herself lately. She's off her food.
BRIDGET: She eats like a horse at Ilam. Everything on her plate.
~~MRS RIEPER: False expectations is what hurts people.~~
~~BRIDGET: Isn't that the truth.~~
MRS RIEPER: She doesn't seem to realise.
BRIDGET: You don't at that age. *She gives* MRS RIEPER *an envelope.* You can rip it up if you like. It's only schoolgirl drivel.
MRS RIEPER: Thank you.
BRIDGET: I won't keep you then. Afternoon.
MRS RIEPER: Good afternoon.

> BRIDGET *goes out.* MRS RIEPER *looks at the envelope debating whether to open it.* PAULINE *and* JULIET *continue writing in their diaries.*

PAULINE: Suddenly the means of ridding myself of the obstacle occurs to me.
JULIET: . . . I see the faint shadow of a solution . . . the faintest of shadows, there on the horizon.
PAULINE: I will not tell Deborah of my plans—yet.
JULIET: I will not say anything to Gina—yet. She must come to see its inevitability herself.
PAULINE: The last fate I wish to meet is one in Borstal.

> MRS RIEPER *hands* PAULINE *the envelope and the record.*

Scene Five

The courtroom.

BROWN: Early this year Dr Hulme decided to resign from his position as Rector of Canterbury College.
BRIDGET: He was forced to resign. Let's keep the record straight.
BROWN: For professional and domestic reasons he decided to return to England, taking his daughter Juliet to South Africa on the way. Circumstances in his home were not too happy.

The Hulmes' lounge.

BRIDGET *observes* WALTER PERRY *kissing* HILDA.

BRIDGET: She met Mister Perry at Marriage Guidance—which just goes to show, doesn't it? *She goes out.*
PERRY: I can't stay.
HILDA: Why not? Henry won't be home for an hour.
PERRY: I think we should wait until you've talked to him.
HILDA: Oh, for God's sake, Walter.
PERRY: I think he suspects.
HILDA: Henry wouldn't know if the house was on fire.
PERRY: You said you'd tell him.
HILDA: I'm trying to! He avoids me. He comes home late, he leaves early.
PERRY: Just tell him.
HILDA: It's all very well for you to say.

They kiss again.

You could live in the flat you know.
PERRY: Bridget lives in the flat.
HILDA: I'll give her notice. It's perfectly natural we should offer you hospitality. After all, we've got an empty flat and no one likes being in a hotel room.
PERRY: You don't have an empty flat.
HILDA: But I could have one.
PERRY: What about Henry? He trusts me.
HILDA: Henry! He runs with the hares and hunts with the hounds.
PERRY: What a fiasco.
HILDA: Don't worry about him. He'll find another job.
PERRY: The loyal wife.
HILDA: I've done my best.
PERRY: Maybe we should wait. Let things settle down.
HILDA: Fine. If that's what you want.
PERRY: I want what's best for all of us.
HILDA: There is no best for all of us. Somebody's got to lose and, by God, this time it's not going to be me.
PERRY: He is a friend of mine Hilda. Be reasonable.
HILDA: I'm past reason. How do you think I feel, stuck here in this God-forsaken country while you two whitter on, business as usual? I can't eat, I can't sleep, I can't think—
PERRY: I'm only saying we owe it to him to—

HILDA: Make up your mind! Choose! Choose now, and if you don't choose me, then push off!

> BRIDGET *enters the room, then backs away before the lovers see her.*

PERRY: Darling, don't. I'll take care of everything. I promise I will. But tell him the truth first. For me.

Scene Six

The Hulmes' dining room.

BRIDGET *lays the table and lights the candles.* HENRY HULME *enters.*

HENRY: Good evening, Mrs O'Malley.
BRIDGET: Evening, Dr Hulme.
HENRY: What's the occasion?
BRIDGET: Mrs Hulme said she wished to dine alone with you. She's putting the little one to bed.
HENRY: Sounds ominous. Where's Juliet?
BRIDGET: Upstairs with Pauline.
HENRY: Doesn't that girl ever go home?
BRIDGET: If you'll excuse me I'll see to the roast.
HENRY: Please don't let me stand in the way of your rendezvous with the roast. But what about slipping me a water biscuit on the sly? I'm famished.
BRIDGET: Certainly, Dr Hulme.

> BRIDGET *goes out.* HENRY *amuses himself passing his finger through the candle flame.* HILDA *enters.*

HILDA: Hello, Henry.
HENRY: I must teach Juliet how to do this one day. Pass through the flames without getting burnt.
HILDA, *sitting down*: Did you have a pleasant day?
HENRY: Not particularly.

> BRIDGET *enters with a packet of water biscuits.* HENRY *scoops up a handful.*

Thank you, Mrs O'Malley. I'm indebted to you eternally.

HILDA: Bridget. The soup please.

> BRIDGET *goes out.*

HENRY, *eating the crackers*: Blame me if you must blame someone. Hunger won out over protocol.
HILDA: Quite.
HENRY: I've been thinking . . .

> BRIDGET *brings out the soup.*

HILDA: Thank you.
HENRY: . . . if you could learn to shave with both hands using two razors you could halve your shaving time.
HILDA: Henry.
HENRY: Mm?
HILDA: I'm in love with Walter Perry.
HENRY: Lathering apart, shaving takes about two and a half minutes so, theoretically, one could save seven hours and four minutes of valuable time per year.
HILDA: I haven't slept with him yet but I intend to do so tomorrow night.
HENRY: Is that so? I wish you'd tell Bridget not to serve the soup cold.
HILDA: I think we should . . . we must finish.
HENRY: I really don't know whether I could learn to shave with two hands this late in the piece.
HILDA: Stop it! Stop playing this childish game.
HENRY: Might I suggest I prefer my game to yours?
HILDA: I want him to live in the flat.
HENRY: No. Not in the flat. Bad idea.
HILDA: Why?
HENRY: My dear, you amaze me. People will talk.
HILDA: There'll be no proof.
HENRY: Think of your reputation—and mine.
HILDA: I didn't think you cared about that kind of thing.
HENRY: Your timing is abysmal.
HILDA: I'm sorry to do this to you Henry. I've tried to make you happy.
HENRY: A lovely speech my dear. First prize.
HILDA: We don't bring out the best in each other.

HENRY: A rather sad summation of our years together don't you think?
HILDA: Yes.
HENRY: It's a point of view one could argue with.
HILDA: But one won't.
HENRY: You seem to have made up your mind.
HILDA: I simply can't bear it any longer.

The moment of reconciliation passes.

HENRY: Are you going to eat something?
HILDA: I'm not hungry.
HENRY: You look disappointed somehow. What did you want me to do? Challenge Sir Walter to a duel?
HILDA: No.
HENRY: I'm giving you what you want. It is what you want, isn't it?
HILDA: Yes.
HENRY: I'm prepared to be civilised. Help yourself, Walter. Eat my roast beef. Roger my wife—

HILDA *storms out.* HENRY *breaks down once she is gone.*

✷ Scene Seven

The courtroom.

BROWN: While at Ilam the girls were often left alone. They spent their time locked away ~~in Juliet Hulme's bedroom~~, scribbling in exercise books various effusions they called novels and making plans for their life together in the future.
BRIDGET: They were courting Lucifer and nobody knew—or cared.

JULIET's *bedroom.*

PAULINE *and* JULIET *are dressed in black outfits and hats pinched from* HILDA's *wardrobe. A shrine to Mario Lanza is set up with Plasticine figures of all the saints. The girls move ceremoniously around the room as a recording of Mario Lanza singing 'I'll walk with God' from* The Student Prince *plays.* JULIET *proposes a toast.*

JULIET: To 'HE'.
PAULINE: Mario Lanza.
JULIET: Happy birthday and many happy returns!

They drink.

PAULINE: May I propose another toast?
JULIET: You may.
PAULINE: To all our saints. Our one true family.
JULIET: To the saints!

They drink again.

PAULINE: Do you think Mario would be terribly jealous if we elevated James to the gods right now?
JULIET: I don't think he would object—would you, Mario mio? *She kisses his face on a record cover. He says no. Begin the ascent.*

PAULINE *brings a photo of James Mason to* JULIET.

PAULINE: Fair goddess, I bring 'HIM' before you that he may ascend from the ranks of the saints to dwell in the temple of the gods and live for evermore in our hearts.

The girls intone.

JULIET: James Mason.
PAULINE: Born Huddersfield, England, 5 May 1909.
JULIET: Discovered by Al Parker who became his agent in . . .
PAULINE: 1938.
JULIET: Don't tell me! I do know. *Pause.* Films.
PAULINE: *Late Extra.*
JULIET *Troubled Waters.*
PAULINE *The Man in Grey.*
JULIET: *Fanny by Gaslight.*
PAULINE *The Seventh Veil.*
JULIET *Caught.*
PAULINE *Madame Bovary.*
JULIET: *East Side—*
PAULINE *West Side.*
JULIET: *Pandora and the Flying Dutchman.*
PAULINE: You forgot *The Restless Moment!*
JULIET: I did not. I hate Joan Bennett. I left it out on purpose.

PAULINE: Sorry.
JULIET: James will have to horsewhip you for that.

> JULIET *playfully lashes out at* PAULINE, *speeding up her litany and erotically tickling her.* PAULINE *shrieks.*

Pandora and the Flying Dutchman, The Desert Fox, Lady Possessed, Prisoner of Zenda.
PAULINE, *breathless*: *Secret Sharer, Wicked Lady, Juliet, Portrait of a Murderer*!
JULIET: Go on.
PAULINE: I can't. You know I'm ticklish.
JULIET: What will James say? You're putting him in a very foul temper.
PAULINE: Oh James darling. Don't be cruel.
JULIET: There is only one way to silence such foolishness.
PAULINE, *coyly*: Yes?

> JULIET *kisses* PAULINE *passionately à la James Mason.*

My darling.

> *They disentangle themselves.*

JULIET: I can see your little brain whirling. Tell me.
PAULINE: We've got to do something if our quest for James is going to amount to anything.
JULIET: If only we had some money.
PAULINE: You could find a publisher in New York.
JULIET: And an agent in Hollywood.
PAULINE: *Vendetta Rides Again*! James would be so perfect as Roland.
JULIET: But who would play Carmelita?
PAULINE: You!
JULIET: Do you think?
PAULINE: You're exactly right for the part. An icy blonde—
JULIET:—with a heart of fire.
PAULINE: You'd have to make love to James on the beach.
JULIET: I'd use a double.
PAULINE: Ooh, I wouldn't.
JULIET: Can you see me lying in the nuddy on the sand?
PAULINE: A crab might walk up and bite your bum!

JULIET: Or Jamesy's you-know-what!
PAULINE: Ooh, disgusting!

    BRIDGET *enters.*

BRIDGET: It's me. I'm collectin' the dirty dishes and the washin'. *She tidies the room.*
JULIET: If only we had money. We need at least a hundred pounds. What about . . . prostitution?

    BRIDGET *crosses herself.*

PAULINE: Brilliant!
JULIET: We could solicit in the Square.
PAULINE: How much do you think we'd get?
JULIET: Ten pounds a pop for me, maybe eight for you. Oh, for God's sake Bridget, don't look so Catholic. This is a theoretical discussion only, isn't it Gina?
PAULINE: Completely theoretical.
BRIDGET: I shouldn't need to be collecting these dirty cups and plates every afternoon. You've both got two good legs to walk on.
JULIET: Bridget approves of our legs!
PAULINE: Oooh!
BRIDGET: Cut your filthy talk and give me a hand.
JULIET: We'll tidy up in a minute.
BRIDGET: If I don't do it myself it'll never get done.
JULIET: Suit yourself.
BRIDGET: Humph.
JULIET: Are you going to town this afternoon?
BRIDGET: You've run out of favours from me.
JULIET: My library books are overdue.
BRIDGET: Let Pauline drop them off.
JULIET: Pauline's busy.
BRIDGET: So am I.
JULIET: Come on Bridget. I'll get a fine otherwise.
BRIDGET: You should have thought of that before.
JULIET: It wouldn't be any trouble.
BRIDGET: Not for you it wouldn't.
JULIET: I'm ill Bridget. You have to coddle me a little. *She coughs pathetically.*

BRIDGET: Where are they?
JULIET: You're a darling.
BRIDGET: I haven't said 'yes' yet.
JULIET: But you're going to. Aren't you?
BRIDGET: Put them in a neat pile on the sideboard downstairs and wipe that smirk off your face.
JULIET: Thank you very much.
BRIDGET: And just watch yourself. You're getting out of hand lately. Both of you. *She goes.*
PAULINE, *mocking her*: You're getting out of hand!
JULIET: Did you see the way I did it? Twisted her right round my little finger?
PAULINE: What if she tells your mother about our discussions?
JULIET: Mummy won't listen. She knows Bridget's a religious maniac.
PAULINE: She's a busy-body of the first order.
JULIET: Maybe a little rearranging of the truth is necessary.
PAULINE: She doesn't know her place any more.
JULIET: Perhaps it's time to take action.
PAULINE: I think so.

The girls assume their mock voices.

JULIET: The china shepherdess was one thing, but my gold locket! Our housekeeper is a thief.
PAULINE: She can't be trusted, Mrs Hulme. It's sad but true.
JULIET: My pearl earrings are gone too.
PAULINE: Not your pearls!
JULIET: Mummy, you've simply got to do something.
PAULINE: I completely agree with Deborah.
JULIET, *in her normal voice*: That's solved then.
PAULINE: You always know what has to be done.
JULIET: Yes, I do.
PAULINE: How many commandments have we broken now?
JULIET: Let me get my diary. We're making good progress. Lying, stealing, false gods . . . coveting your neighbour's wife—we'll have to let Mr Perry be our stand-in for that one.
PAULINE: Do you have any proof yet?
JULIET: No. But my instincts tell me it won't be long.
PAULINE: Good. What about . . . ?

ACT I

JULIET: The ultimate?
PAULINE: *Portrait of a Murderer.*
JULIET: I was wondering when you would ask.
PAULINE: I'm asking.
JULIET: I can read you like a book Gina. *She puts her hands on* PAULINE. A presence is troubling you.
PAULINE: Yes.
JULIET: Someone is standing in your way. Someone very close and very, very loathsome.
PAULINE: Yes.
JULIET: You cannot become what you are meant to be in the face of this obstacle.
PAULINE: Yes. Yes.
JULIET: Something has to be done.
PAULINE: She's taking me out of school and sending me to secretarial college.
JULIET: She can't! What about your exams?
PAULINE: Mother has my life planned. Death by degree at Digby's.
JULIET: Fight it. Fight her. You must.
PAULINE, *bowing*: My Lord.

Scene Eight

The courtroom.

BROWN: Pauline Parker's mother was known as Mrs Rieper, having lived for more than twenty years as the wife of Mr Herbert Rieper who unfortunately was unable to marry her. No one had any inkling of this, least of all the accused Parker. Please put the relationship of the father and the mother out of your mind. I emphasise that, although they were not legally married, they were thoroughly good decent people, good parents and devoted to their children.

1954. The Riepers' lounge, evening.

MRS RIEPER *is knitting,* MR RIEPER *is cleaning the canary's cage, and* PAULINE *is writing in her diary.*

PAULINE: As usual I woke up and managed to write a considerable amount. I felt depressed at the thought of the day. There seems to be no possibility of Mother relenting and allowing me to go out to see Deborah tomorrow. She is most—

MRS RIEPER: Did you put the kettle on Pauline? It should be whistling by now.

Silence.

Pauline, I'm talking to you.

PAULINE: I'm in the middle of a sentence.

MR RIEPER: It's all right Mum. I'm up. *He goes into the kitchen.*

PAULINE: —she is most unreasonable. Why could not Mother die? Dozens of people are dying. Thousands are dying every day so why not Mother, and Father too?

MRS RIEPER: Your father's been on his feet all day. I wish, just once, you'd offer to lend a hand without making a fuss.

PAULINE: Who's making a fuss?

MRS RIEPER: Don't give me cheek.

PAULINE: I'm not. I'm trying to concentrate.

MRS RIEPER: Then go upstairs. You're putting a damper on things.

PAULINE: Thank you very much.

MRS RIEPER: I don't like to see your father waiting on you.

PAULINE: Oh all right! *Calling*: Dad! Come sit down. Mother thinks you're too decrepit to be in the kitchen.

MR RIEPER *appears with food for the canary.*

MR RIEPER: How's that?

PAULINE *storms into the kitchen.*

PAULINE, *off*: I said I'll make the tea.

MR RIEPER: What was that all about?

MRS RIEPER: Her Majesty objects to lending a hand. Juliet never lifts a finger, so why should she?

MR RIEPER: Not Juliet again.

MRS RIEPER: She didn't say Juliet but I knew that's what she was thinking. What's that in your hand?

MR RIEPER: Lettuce. A lovely bit of lettuce for Billy.

MRS RIEPER: You're not wasting the heart on him are you?

ACT 1

MR RIEPER: Wasting! Nothing but the best for my Billy Boy. Who's a pretty boy then? Come on, sing for your supper.
MRS RIEPER: You'll spoil him.
MR RIEPER: You can't spoil a bird.
MRS RIEPER: He'll pop. He already looks like a little yellow balloon.
MR RIEPER: Billy, did you hear that? Mother'll be putting you on a diet next.

Loud thumps and bangs are heard from the kitchen.

MRS RIEPER: What's that girl doing? You'd think I asked her to clean Buckingham Palace. Pauline!

PAULINE *appears with a tea tray.*

PAULINE: What?
MRS RIEPER: Is it that hard to make a quiet cup of tea?
PAULINE: Yes.
MR RIEPER: Set the tray down before you drop it. I'll pour.
PAULINE: Ta.
MR RIEPER: What's this one about?
PAULINE: Roland and Carmelita. There's also a horse called Vendetta.
MRS RIEPER: Sounds a bit far-fetched to me.
PAULINE: But you don't read much, Mother.
MRS RIEPER: I've read enough to know what far-fetched is. What was the name of the film we saw where everyone was called something impossible? All Spanishy . . . Guadalupe and Mirandella . . .
MR RIEPER: You've got me. Something Rio.
MRS RIEPER: Rio Rita? It was far-fetched anyway but it did have some lovely tunes.

MR RIEPER *begins whistling.*

PAULINE: Dad! Don't start Billy up again. His twittering drives me mad.
MRS RIEPER: Then may I suggest Her Majesty retires to her own chambers?
MR RIEPER: Leave her be Mum. It's nice to have her working downstairs for a change.

PAULINE: It would suit us all if I went away with the Hulmes. Then I'd be out of your life for good.

MR RIEPER: Let's not go through all this again.

MRS RIEPER: You're too young to be leaving home. You've no way of keeping yourself. If you think the world's going to pay you to write about some Italian horse you've got another think coming. You'll end up washing dishes in some hotel unless you finish at Digby's.

PAULINE: I don't want to be a secretary.

MRS RIEPER: It's only for a few years until you have a family.

PAULINE: I don't want a bloody family!

MRS RIEPER: Pauline!

PAULINE: Sorry.

MRS RIEPER: You might be able to travel and even meet up with Juliet one day. But you can't tag around the world after her.

PAULINE: I've already explained a hundred times the Hulmes would help me out until I found a job.

MRS RIEPER: Mrs Hulme told me they couldn't keep you. She said it as plain as day.

PAULINE: When?

MRS RIEPER: I talked to her. On the phone last week. And I saw Dr Hulme before that.

PAULINE: You went out to Ilam?

MRS RIEPER: No. He came here.

PAULINE: You've got no right!

MRS RIEPER: This is my house and I'll see who I like.

PAULINE: You're hateful! I hate you.

MR RIEPER: Now Pauline, there's no reason to be upset—

PAULINE: Stop trying to interfere with my life! I was getting on perfectly well with the Hulmes and now you've spoiled it.

MRS RIEPER: Mrs Hulme told me she has never encouraged you or Juliet to think you could stay together. Juliet's going away with her family partly to get away from you.

PAULINE: She's not! It's a lie!

MRS RIEPER: The Hulmes don't like you and Juliet spending so much time together and neither—

PAULINE, *screaming*: It's a bloody filthy lie! I'm one of the family! They want me! *She runs out of the room.*

MRS RIEPER: If I thought it would do any good to take the back of my hand to her, I would. Put the cover over Billy. He's seen enough for one night.
MR RIEPER: You know what they say Mum.
MRS RIEPER: Do I?
MR RIEPER: This too shall pass, eh? This too shall pass.

Scene Nine

The Hulmes' lounge.

HILDA, *calling out to* BRIDGET *who is in the kitchen*: Bridget? Bridget, can you come here for a moment?
BRIDGET, *calling*: I'm up to my elbows in soapy water. I won't be a tick. *She enters, wiping her hands on her apron.*
HILDA: Sit down, please.
BRIDGET: Don't mind if I do. I always get a crick in my back bending over that sink.

Silence.

Is there something wrong?
HILDA: No.
BRIDGET: What are you looking at me like that for?
HILDA: Bridget. Mrs O'Malley. You've given us very good service over the past . . .
BRIDGET: One and a half years.
HILDA: One and a half years. You're making this very difficult for me, wringing your hands like that.
BRIDGET: I'm drying them. If it's about the roast it's not my fault. The oven's playing up again.
HILDA: The roast is not the issue.
BRIDGET: You'd never have known it the way the boss was carrying on.
HILDA: We're not entertaining as much as I thought and—
BRIDGET: I can't cook properly unless you get the oven seen to. It's as simple as that.
HILDA: It's not the cooking.
BRIDGET: Well then?

HILDA: I've noticed a few things aren't where they usually are. The shepherdess on the mantelpiece, the pewter case in my bedroom . . .
BRIDGET: Are you accusing me of stealing?
HILDA: They are missing.
BRIDGET: Have you looked in Juliet's bedroom?
HILDA: No. Juliet's locket's gone too.
BRIDGET: Try the bottom drawer of her wardrobe.
HILDA: Oh? Well . . . maybe she borrowed . . .
BRIDGET: I'd never touch anything that wasn't mine.
HILDA: Yes. I'm not suggesting that. That's why I hadn't said anything. I knew there was some mistake.
BRIDGET: A prank more likely.
HILDA: I must speak to Juliet.
BRIDGET: You must. And to Pauline.
HILDA: I don't appreciate that tone of voice, Bridget.
BRIDGET: What tone?
HILDA: You seem to take it upon yourself to pass judgement—
BRIDGET: I never said—
HILDA: All right then, it's the way you radiate disapproval. At me.
BRIDGET: You want the flat.
HILDA: As a matter of fact I do.
BRIDGET: For Mr Perry.
HILDA: Mr Perry is a very dear friend and it's most uncomfortable for him to be living semi-permanently in a hotel room.
BRIDGET: Aye.
HILDA: Dr Hulme and I have decided to offer him the flat. I'm sorry. I don't wish to discuss it any further.
BRIDGET: You're firing me?
HILDA: I'm very sorry, Mrs O'Malley. Circumstances have changed somewhat. Good afternoon.

  HILDA *leaves*.

BRIDGET: All that talk—you must call me Hilda. She didn't have any qualms about ditching me. She wanted the flat for purposes of fornication, pure and simple.

⭐ Scene Ten

A moonlit night. The temple of Raphael and Pan in the Hulmes' garden.

JULIET *and* PAULINE *are performing a ritual in front of the altar.*

JULIET and PAULINE, *chanting together*:
   There live among us two dutiful daughters
   Behind their masks are two beautiful daughters
   The most glorious beings in creation.
   They'd be the pride and joy of any nation.
   You cannot know or try to guess
   The sweet soothingness of their caress.
   The outstanding genius of this pair
   Is understood by few, they are so rare.
   Compared with these two all men are fools
   The world is most honoured that they should rule.
   Above us these goddesses reign on high . . .

   PAULINE *begins to cry.*

JULIET: What's wrong?
PAULINE: I can't help it.
JULIET: Darling, don't.
PAULINE: I don't know what to do.
JULIET: Did you have another fight?
PAULINE: Mother said she couldn't wait until you were gone.
JULIET: Did she?
PAULINE: Every day is one day closer to losing you.
JULIET: But you're coming with me.
PAULINE: How can I? I don't even have a passport.
JULIET: That's a detail! Listen. Once we're in New York we'll find an agent for our novels . . . then we'll go to Hollywood . . . we'll meet people and everything will fall into place.
PAULINE: I've got no money.
JULIET: We'll find some. *She strokes* PAULINE's *hair.* Look at the sky.
PAULINE: It's too big. It confuses me.

JULIET: I'll look at it for you then. I will be your map of heaven. Close your eyes...imagine the Fourth World...our paradise ...it's out there...beyond the stars waiting for us to claim it.

A glimmer of the Fourth World flares up then fades.

This world is a cruel place, Gina. Don't you ever forget that.

PAULINE: What are we going to do?

JULIET: When I sold my useless horse to Mr Perry he gave me fifty pounds.

PAULINE: Fifty pounds isn't enough.

JULIET: Have you ever heard of extortion? Mister Bloody Perry's doing it with Mummy.

PAULINE: He is?

JULIET: He is. And if he wants to continue—without Daddy knowing—it will cost him. Twenty pounds a poke!

They giggle.

That should do nicely, don't you think?

PAULINE: But what about my mother?

JULIET: She can't stop you.

PAULINE: Mother won't let me go with you no matter what. She's immovable.

JULIET: I thought we had an understanding. If things come to that.

PAULINE: Do we?

JULIET: Courage my love. *She picks up a sharp stone.* Give me your hands.

PAULINE *holds out her hands.*

Swear you will follow me to Hell and back if I command it.

PAULINE: Where you go, I go also.

JULIET *cuts* PAULINE.

JULIET: Now cut me.

PAULINE: Deborah!

JULIET: Diello casts out the weak. He vomits the lukewarm out of his mouth.

PAULINE *takes the stone from* JULIET *and cuts her.*

PAULINE: My Lord.
JULIET: Our blood has been shed to uphold our sacred vow.
PAULINE: Together unto eternity.

> They smear blood on each other's hands.

JULIET: Are you thinking what I'm thinking, darling Gina?
PAULINE: Yes. I've been thinking it for ages.
JULIET: Snap?
PAULINE, *whispering*: Snap.
JULIET: I worship the power of these lovely two
           With that adoring love known to so few.
PAULINE: 'Tis indeed a miracle one must feel
           That two such heavenly creatures are real.
JULIET: We will not be parted.

Scene Eleven

April 1954. PERRY's flat, 2 a.m.

HILDA *and* PERRY *are in bed.* HILDA *pours* PERRY *and herself a drink.*

HILDA: To July third when this pathetic charade is over.
PERRY: Henry's bought his ticket?
HILDA: London via South Africa. He's prancing about like a satyr in anticipation. I think he's taken a mistress he's so excited.
PERRY: Henry with a mistress?
HILDA: His secretary.
PERRY: You're jealous.
HILDA: I'm not. Well, maybe a little.
PERRY: How would you like to marry me?
HILDA: I'm tempted.
PERRY: Are you?
HILDA: Yes. Very.

> HILDA *pulls* PERRY *down on the bed. They begin to make love.*

PERRY: You greedy old thing.

> JULIET *enters.*

JULIET: Oh, so there you are. Hello.
HILDA: What are you doing?
JULIET: I heard noises.
HILDA: Mr Perry's ill.

    JULIET *begins to laugh.*

I think you should go back to bed.
JULIET: I've been standing outside the door for an hour.
HILDA: Do as I say.
JULIET: I knew I'd catch you out eventually. Gina and I need a hundred pounds.
HILDA: Don't be absurd.
JULIET: It's two o'clock in the morning, Mummy.
HILDA: How dare you! Mr Perry is in terrible pain and I was getting him a cup of tea.
JULIET: Everyone lies to me.
PERRY: Your mother is in a very difficult situation. Do you understand what I'm saying?
JULIET: I think I do.
PERRY: You're an intelligent girl. Don't make things worse.
JULIET: Does Daddy know?

    Silence.

Does he?
HILDA: Yes he does.
JULIET: Are you going to get a divorce?
HILDA: I don't know.
JULIET: Are we going back to England?
HILDA: I don't know.
JULIET: You don't know much, do you.
HILDA: I want you to go back to bed right now. Say good night to Mr Perry.
JULIET, *cuttingly polite*: Good night, Mr Perry. *She goes out.*
PERRY: She's old enough to understand.
HILDA: Don't tell me how to raise my children.

Scene Twelve

August 1954. The courtroom.

BROWN *is cross-examining* HILDA.

BRIDGET: By April 1954 Juliet knew exactly what wickedness her mother and Mr Perry were up to. It all came out at the trial. Hilda had to testify, and there she stood on the witness stand, without the protection of her husband's fancy prefix, all white-knuckled and pale-cheeked. God forgive me, I enjoyed every minute of her humiliation.

BROWN: At first the girls' writings were merely extravagant and grandiose but later murder, suicide, imprisonment, bloodshed and sudden death entered in to a disproportionate degree?

HILDA: I . . . yes.

BROWN: You have read Parker's 1954 diary?

HILDA: I have.

BROWN: It is a truthful document?

HILDA: I find it difficult to say how much is true.

BRIDGET: Oh, aye. Very difficult.

BROWN: I will read you the diary entry from April 23.

'April 23. Last night Deborah told me some stupendous news. She awoke at 2 a.m. and went into her mother's room. She could not find her so she crept as stealthily as she could into Mr Perry's flat and stole upstairs. Mr Perry and Mrs Hulme were in bed "drinking tea"! Deborah felt an hysterical tendency to giggle. She was shaking with shock and emotion although she knew she had known what she would find. Her mother said, "I suppose you want an explanation." "Yes I do," replied Deborah. "Well you see we are in love," her mother replied. She explained that Dr Hulme knew all about it and they intended to live as a threesome. Deborah told them about our desire to go to America though she could not explain our reasons of course. Mr Perry gave her a hundred pounds. Everyone is being frightfully decent about everything.'

BROWN: Is this diary entry anywhere near the truth?

HILDA: It is nowhere near the truth. The entry is a work of fiction.

BROWN: Are you certain?
HILDA: Yes I am.
BRIDGET: You're telling the truth and pigs can fly, eh Hilda?
BROWN: Thank you Mrs Hulme.

> HILDA *goes out. She sees* BRIDGET *and deliberately snubs her.*

Early in June when the date of Dr Hulme's departure had been fixed the accused coldly and calculatedly formed a plan to kill Mrs Parker. Ten days before the murder, Parker was allowed to stay with Juliet Hulme for a week. She returned home on Sunday evening and was particularly pleasant.

⭒ Scene Thirteen

June 1954. The Riepers' lounge, evening.

PAULINE *is writing in her diary. Her parents are in the room.*

PAULINE: Our main idea for the day was to moider Mother. This notion is not a new one but this time it is a definite plan which we intend to carry out. We have worked it out carefully and are both thrilled with the idea. Naturally we feel a trifle nervous, but the pleasure of anticipation is great.

In her own bedroom, JULIET *is writing in her diary.*

JULIET: Gina is very excited, as am I. At last we begin to move towards the final culmination of our dreams. Our consciences are clear. Great love requires great sacrifice.

The Riepers' lounge.

PAULINE: I shall not write the plan down here as I shall write it up when we carry it out—I hope. Peculiarly enough I have no qualms of conscience.

> *A tea kettle whistles off-stage.* PAULINE *shuts her diary and goes to the kitchen with a spring in her step.*

MR RIEPER: Did you have a nice time at the Hulmes', love?
PAULINE: Oh yes. I had a lovely week, thank you. *Off*: I'll make the tea.

ACT I

MR RIEPER: That would be grand. *To* MRS RIEPER: She's bright tonight.
MRS RIEPER: She wants something, that's why.
PAULINE, *off*: Do we have any loaf?
MRS RIEPER: In the tin.
MR RIEPER: What about a nice bit of apple for Billy?
MRS RIEPER: But don't cut one up unless it's bruised.
PAULINE, *off*: All right!
MRS RIEPER: Butter wouldn't melt in her mouth.
MR RIEPER: Give her a chance.
MRS RIEPER: Two weeks, then Juliet's gone.
MR RIEPER: Do you think we should have them around to say goodbye?
MRS RIEPER: A phone call will do. Lady Muck has a busy social calendar.
MR RIEPER: I'll be a happy man when all this is over.
PAULINE, *returning*: Here we are. Buttered fruit loaf and apple for Billy.
MR RIEPER: Aren't you a wonder.
PAULINE, *setting the tray down*: More milk?
MRS RIEPER: No, that's fine.
PAULINE: Dad?
MR RIEPER: Not for me.

Silence.

Something on your mind love?
PAULINE: Not really . . . except Juliet and I were wondering if we couldn't do something together before she goes. She wants to say goodbye.
MRS RIEPER: Well, well.
PAULINE: It's less than two weeks.
MR RIEPER: You girls do something together.
MRS RIEPER: Were you thinking of a meal out?
PAULINE: How about a picnic?
MRS RIEPER: In the middle of winter?
PAULINE: A walk then.
MRS RIEPER: There's not much to see in the gardens this time of year.
PAULINE: We were thinking Victoria Park might be fun.

MRS RIEPER: It's a bit out of the way.
PAULINE: We could stop at the tea kiosk. The view's lovely.
MRS RIEPER: I'm not walking anywhere in the rain.
PAULINE: It won't rain.
MRS RIEPER: The weather does what it likes regardless of Juliet Hulme.
PAULINE: It should clear by Tuesday.
MRS RIEPER: All right. All right. Tell her to come round for lunch first. Then we can all say goodbye.

The phone rings. PAULINE *leaps up.*

PAULINE: I'll get it.
MR RIEPER: If it's Juliet don't talk all night.

While PAULINE *and* JULIET *talk* MR *and* MRS RIEPER *dance to the radio.*

PAULINE: Deborah?
JULIET: Hello, darling. You sound puffed.
PAULINE: She's agreed. This Tuesday.
JULIET: I knew she would. She likes me.
PAULINE: But she won't go if it's raining. It has to be fine.
JULIET: Don't worry.
PAULINE: I'm not. I'm just a bit Night-Before-Christmassy, you know?
JULIET: Mmm. What's happening tomorrow?
PAULINE: I said I'd help her with the housework.
JULIET: Very good.
PAULINE: When she goes out to do the shopping I'll make the sandbag.
JULIET: I've been thinking about that. What if it only stuns her? We need something more final.
PAULINE: A knife?
JULIET: Don't be daft. It's still got to look like an accident. I was thinking of a brick. Half a brick in a stocking so we can swing it.

Silence.

Gina?
PAULINE: I'm here.

JULIET: Is that too awful?
PAULINE: Oh no. I think it's a marvellous idea.
JULIET: It would be the most humane thing. One sharp blow. Or maybe two. We could each take a turn. Fair's fair.
PAULINE: Absolutely. Where will I get a brick?
JULIET: I'll bring one.
PAULINE: And the stocking?
JULIET: Pinch one of your sister's. No point in spoiling a good pair.

Silence.

Are you all right?
PAULINE: How hot is it in South Africa?
JULIET: It's perfect. Very temperate.
PAULINE: Once we get settled I'll save up and send my father the fare. Or do you think he'd prefer to go back to Australia?
JULIET: Whatever. We've got to do it. You haven't changed your mind have you?
PAULINE: I'd die without you.
JULIET: The same. Don't cry. You're not crying, are you?
PAULINE: I never cry. You know that.
JULIET: If something happens and we don't get to South Africa right away we'll still be together.
PAULINE: As long as they put us in the same room. Or would it be a cell?
JULIET: They don't have cells anymore. Mental institutions are terribly enlightened these days.
PAULINE: Straitjackets by Dior.
JULIET: You toad. Think of it as an experience on the way to Paradise.
PAULINE: I really do loathe her.
JULIET: How's she been?
PAULINE: She knitted herself a cardy while I was away. It's a revolting fuchsia colour.
JULIET: No quarrels?
PAULINE: She wants to but I don't let her. I'm oozing charm and tact.
JULIET: Good girl. How's Billy?
PAULINE: Scuttling back and forth in his cage with his stupid toenails scratching.

JULIET: Ugh!
PAULINE: I swear that bird is demented.
JULIET: Think of it as a release.
PAULINE: A blessed release.
JULIET: I'd better go.
PAULINE: I'll ring you tomorrow afternoon.
JULIET: Good. We need to make certain everything's in order. Farewell.
PAULINE: Bon soir.

> PAULINE *returns to the lounge. She watches her parents dance.*

MR RIEPER: You can't!
MRS RIEPER: I can hear it sloshing! Every time you twirl!
MR RIEPER: You're mad.
MRS RIEPER: No, really. Listen. *She puts her ear on his stomach.* Now who would have thought?
MR RIEPER: You should be gazing tenderly in my eyes and here you are listening to tea slosh around in my stomach.

> MRS RIEPER *sings to the radio.*

MRS RIEPER: I've always liked this tune. *She sees* PAULINE *and stops dancing.* Well, all settled?

> PAULINE *nods.*

MR RIEPER: Come and have a dance with your dear old Dad then. Come on.

> *He holds out his arms to* PAULINE. *She walks out of the room.*

Scene Fourteen

The courtroom.

BRIDGET: It's little ordinary details that get to you. We sat there in the public gallery, shifting in our seats while Mr Brown described the final journey.
BROWN: At about 11 a.m. on June 23rd, Dr Hulme drove his

ACT 1

    daughter to the vicinity of the Parker home in Gloucester Street.
BRIDGET: By all acounts they had a jolly family luncheon.
BROWN: Shortly after 2.30 p.m., Mrs Parker and the two accused were in Victoria Park, up on the Port Hills behind the city. There is a tea kiosk there where they were served with tea and soft drinks.
BRIDGET: Tea, soft drinks . . . and blood for afters.

Victoria Park Tearooms.

PAULINE, JULIET *and* MRS RIEPER *are finishing afternoon tea. They have coats and bags.*

MRS RIEPER: There's nothing like a hot cup of tea on a cold winter's day. I suppose you're looking forward to your trip?
JULIET: Oh yes. Very much.
MRS RIEPER: I've only been on a ship once. That was coming out from England when I was eighteen. It was terribly exciting—the biggest thing that had ever happened to me.
JULIET: My mother doesn't like it here.
MRS RIEPER: I daresay it takes some getting used to. It's not like home.
JULIET: No.
MRS RIEPER: But it's very clean and bright. There's a lot to be said for New Zealand.

    The girls exchange looks.

PAULINE: Do you want anything more, Mother?
MRS RIEPER: Oh, I couldn't.
JULIET: The cakes were quite nice, considering.

    MRS RIEPER *drains her cup.*

MRS RIEPER: How about you two?
PAULINE: We're fine thank you.
MRS RIEPER: Perhaps we should go then?

    JULIET *takes out a coin purse.*

    No, it's my treat.
JULIET: I don't mind paying.

MRS RIEPER: I insist. After all, it's a special occasion. Now you two, run along. *Confidentially*: I need to spend a penny.
JULIET: Thank you very much then.
PAULINE: Thank you, Mother. We'll wait for you at the top of the track.

> MRS RIEPER *goes out.*

PAULINE: Sometimes she makes me want to scream. *Imitating her mother*: 'I need to spend a penny.'
JULIET: Have you got your shoulder bag?
PAULINE: It's here. Where's the pink stone?
JULIET: In my pocket. *Imitating*: 'It was terribly exciting—the biggest thing that had ever happened to me!'
PAULINE: Come on!

> *They leave the tearooms and meet* MRS RIEPER *walking down the track.*

MRS RIEPER: Isn't it cold! I shouldn't have worn these shoes. My toes feel icy.
PAULINE: Do you want to sit down?
MRS RIEPER: Maybe I will. You two carry on. I'll catch up with you in a minute.
PAULINE: You don't mind?
MRS RIEPER: No. The peace and quiet suit me.

> PAULINE *and* JULIET *walk a little further down the track.*

JULIET: See that bridge? I'll drop it there. I'll turn around and make a sign so you can see the exact spot.
PAULINE: Good. I feel sick.
JULIET: You shouldn't have eaten all those cakes, you guts.
PAULINE: I know.

> *They embrace.*

I'll go back to Mother. See you soon.
JULIET: It's like a film isn't it?
PAULINE: Universal Studios presents—
JULIET: Moidering Mother!

> *They try to stifle their laughter.*

ACT 1   57

PAULINE: Shhh!
JULIET: I think I'm hysterical.
PAULINE: Calm down, Darling. We have to concentrate.

> *They part.* JULIET *goes to the bridge and drops the pink stone.* PAULINE *notes its position then returns to her mother.*

MRS RIEPER: There you are. Where's Juliet?
PAULINE: She went on ahead.
MRS RIEPER: Oh?
PAULINE: She said she'll meet up with us back at the tearooms.

> MRS RIEPER *takes* PAULINE*'s hands.*

MRS RIEPER: Goodness me! I told you you should have worn gloves.
PAULINE: I'm all right.
MRS RIEPER: You're not too upset about her going?
PAULINE: I'll survive.
MRS RIEPER: Of course you will. Things have a way of working out.
PAULINE: Shall we go? I'll follow you in case you slip.
MRS RIEPER: I'm not that ancient.

> MRS RIEPER *and* PAULINE *begin walking towards the bridge.* JULIET *is beyond it, hiding.*

PAULINE: Look, Mother. What's that?
MRS RIEPER: What?
PAULINE: On the ground. Something pink.

> MRS RIEPER *bends down.* PAULINE *takes the brick out of her shoulder bag.*

MRS RIEPER: It's some kind of stone. It looks like a bit off a necklace . . .

> PAULINE *silently raises the brick.*

Maybe it's part of a charm bracelet . . .

> PAULINE *strikes her mother.* JULIET *comes running to assist her. The Fourth World envelops them.*

✫ Scene Fifteen

Outside the tea kiosk.

PAULINE's *and* JULIET's *coats are spattered with blood.*

PAULINE: Remember—it was an accident.
JULIET: She slipped and hit her head on a stone.
PAULINE: On the brick. We have to account for the brick.
JULIET: You've got blood on your face. And your hands.
PAULINE: We've got to get back to the tearooms and say there was an accident.
JULIET: My coat's ruined. I didn't think there would be quite so much blood.
PAULINE: No.
JULIET: It wasn't quite what I expected.
PAULINE: No.
JULIET: You were very brave.
PAULINE: Deborah. We killed her.
JULIET: We had to do it.
PAULINE: We had to.
JULIET: I'm shaking all over.
PAULINE: I'll always love you.
JULIET: Cross your heart?
PAULINE: Cross my heart.
JULIET: And hope to die?
PAULINE: And hope to die.
JULIET: I worship the power of these lovely two
            With that adoring love known to so few.
PAULINE: 'Tis indeed a miracle one must feel
            That two such heavenly creatures are real.
BRIDGET: Forty-five times they hit her. Not once, not twice but forty-five times.

Act Two

Scene One

BRIDGET: This is how I found out. I was doing the potatoes when my neighbour told me there'd been an accident in Victoria Park. I wasn't much interested—some kiddie falling off a swing, I thought. Then she whispers, 'The Hulme girl and her little friend ran into the tea kiosk covered with blood. I thought you'd want to know.' Was I surprised? No. But even so, the hairs on the back of my neck stood up and began marching.

June 22nd. The Hulmes' house. PAULINE *is in the spare bedroom.* HENRY, HILDA, PERRY *and the* POLICE DETECTIVE *are outside the room in a hallway.*

HILDA: As I said, my husband brought Juliet and the Rieper girl straight home after the accident.

The DETECTIVE *addresses* PERRY.

DETECTIVE: What did the girls tell you?
HILDA, *indicating Henry*: Sorry, this is my husband.
DETECTIVE: I beg your pardon.
PERRY: Walter Perry.
DETECTIVE: Senior Sergeant Tate.

They shake hands.

HILDA: Mr Perry is a close family friend.
DETECTIVE, *to Henry*: The girls . . . did either of them say anything significant to you?
HILDA: Only that there'd been a terrible accident. Juliet was quite hysterical.
DETECTIVE: And Pauline?

HILDA: She was calm. Strangely calm.
DETECTIVE, *to Henry*: Is that correct?
HENRY: More or less.
DETECTIVE: And then?
HILDA: I gave both girls a bath.
HENRY: Mr Perry took their coats to the drycleaners.
DETECTIVE: Oh?
HILDA: I was afraid they would stain.

The DETECTIVE *makes a note.*

DETECTIVE: Where are the girls now?
HILDA: Juliet's sleeping. Pauline's in the spare room. Would you like to talk to her?
DETECTIVE: I would, yes.
HENRY: I'll wait downstairs.
HILDA: Please do.

HENRY *goes out.* PERRY, HILDA *and the* POLICE DETECTIVE *go to* PAULINE.

HILDA: This is the police detective, Pauline. Tell him what you told me.
PAULINE: Mother slipped and hit her head on a rock or a stone or something.
DETECTIVE: Where was Juliet?
PAULINE: Six or seven feet ahead of us. Mother's head kept banging. We tried to lift her but we couldn't. There was a half brick lying there.
DETECTIVE: How did you know your mother was dead?
PAULINE: Blood. There was a lot of blood.
DETECTIVE: Did you see a stocking there?
PAULINE, *taken by surprise*: A stocking? No. We didn't take Mother's stockings off. I wasn't wearing stockings, I was wearing sockettes—but I had stockings with me. In my bag. I wiped the blood with them.
DETECTIVE: Pauline, we've reason to believe that Juliet was not present when the fatality occurred.
PAULINE, *realising Juliet has lied*: Not present? Yes. That's right.
DETECTIVE: Listen carefully, Pauline. You are suspected of the murder of your mother. You don't need to say anything but

ACT II

you can make a statement if you wish which will be written down and used in evidence.

PAULINE: I don't want to make a statement. But you can ask me questions.

DETECTIVE: Very well then. Who assaulted your mother?

PAULINE: I did.

DETECTIVE: Why?

PAULINE: If you don't mind I won't answer that question.

DETECTIVE: When did you make up your mind to kill your mother?

PAULINE: A few days ago.

DETECTIVE: Did you tell anyone you were going to do it?

PAULINE: No. Juliet didn't know anything about it. She was out of sight at the time—she'd gone on ahead.

DETECTIVE: What did your mother do when you struck her?

PAULINE: I would rather not answer that question.

DETECTIVE: How often did you hit her?

PAULINE: I don't know, but a great many times I imagine.

DETECTIVE: What did you use?

PAULINE: A half brick inside the foot of a stocking. I took the stockings with me on purpose and I had the brick in my shoulder bag. Juliet didn't know of my intentions and she didn't see me strike my mother.

DETECTIVE: Did you tell Juliet that you killed your mother?

PAULINE: She knew nothing about it.

DETECTIVE: Why did Juliet tell the same story as you to the lady in the tea kiosk?

PAULINE: She was simply copying me. Perhaps she'd suspected what I had done and she didn't want me to get into trouble. *Pause.* As soon as I started to strike my mother I regretted it but I couldn't stop then.

DETECTIVE: Where did you get the brick?

HILDA, *quickly*: She didn't get it here. The girl Rieper took it from home.

DETECTIVE: Is that correct?

PAULINE: That's correct.

DETECTIVE: You'll need to come with me now Pauline. I'm placing you under arrest.

PAULINE: I'd like to speak with Deborah first please.

DETECTIVE: I'm afraid that's not possible.
HILDA: She's sleeping.
PAULINE: Oh. I see. Well, thank you so much for having me then. Good night.

> PAULINE *goes out, followed by the* DETECTIVE.

PERRY: ~~I told you taking those coats to the drycleaners was a mistake. There's nothing to be gained by—~~
HILDA: ~~Walter, please! Let me think!~~

Scene Two

The Riepers' lounge. The same night.

The DETECTIVE *is waiting to search the house.* MR RIEPER *is staring at Billy in the bird cage.*

DETECTIVE: Has he got a name?
MR RIEPER: Billy.
DETECTIVE: Hello, Billy. ~~There's a pretty boy.~~ Can you whistle for me?
MR RIEPER: He only whistles when he's happy.

> *Silence.*

Her bedroom's upstairs. Second on the left. The door's open.
DETECTIVE: Mr Rieper, I'm sorry to be—
MR RIEPER: I know. You're only doing your job.

> *The* DETECTIVE *goes out.* MR RIEPER *gazes at Billy, in shock. The* DETECTIVE *re-enters with an armful of notebooks.*

DETECTIVE: Fourteen notebooks, one scrapbook and a diary. They were lying on the bed. *He reads a page*: 'June 22nd. The day of the Happy Event.' *To* MR RIEPER: You never read this?
MR RIEPER: We didn't think it was honourable to do so.
DETECTIVE, *shutting the diary*: I appreciate your cooperation, sir. We'll be back tomorrow morning. Good night.

Mr Rieper: Good night.

> *The* Detective *goes out.*

> Who would have thought, Billy Boy . . . ? *He covers the cage, weeping.* Jesus Bloody Christ.

⭐ Scene Three

Juliet's *bedroom.* [handwritten: dining room] *The same night.*

Juliet, Hilda *and* Perry *are in the room.*

Juliet: Where's Gina? You promised I could see Gina after the police left.
Perry: She's been arrested.
Juliet: Where's Daddy? I want Daddy.
Hilda: There's nothing he can do.
Juliet: Gina!
Perry: Come on, pull yourself together, Juliet.
Juliet: Don't touch me! You're glad this has happened aren't you? You wanted them to take her away from me.
Perry: Calm down Juliet.
Juliet: I hate you! Gina! Gina!
Hilda: Listen to me. I forbid you to see or speak to that girl ever again.
Juliet: Gina!
Hilda: I said no more!

> *She slaps* Juliet *hard across the face.* Juliet *weeps.* Hilda *embraces her.*

She's a very disturbed girl, Juliet. Very disturbed.
Juliet: Mummy.
Hilda: Yes darling?
Juliet: I did it too. I hit her. Over and over. With the brick.
Hilda: Oh my God.
Juliet: I pushed her face down in the mud until she stopped breathing.
Hilda: Why?
Juliet: I'm sorry. I had to.

> *Silence.*

HILDA: Juliet. Tell me exactly what you've said to the police.
JULIET: I said I heard an argument and when I came back along the track Mrs Rieper was already lying on the ground. I said I thought she'd slipped and fallen.
PERRY: It's better that she tells the truth, Hilda.
HILDA: Don't be a fool. You planned this . . . act . . . with Pauline?
JULIET: Yes.
HILDA: Where's your diary?
JULIET: In the bottom drawer.
HILDA: Get it.
JULIET: But it's everything, not just the moider.
HILDA: Get it.

> JULIET *fetches her diary and gives it to her mother.* HILDA *flicks through it then hands it to* PERRY.

Burn it. Burn it in the incinerator.

> *Perry hesitates, then takes the diary and goes out.*

You must do exactly as I say.
JULIET: I'm frightened.
HILDA: You are a very stupid girl. A stupid, stupid girl.
JULIET: Yes.
HILDA: The police said they'd be back in the morning. Think hard. Is there anything else that shouldn't be here?
JULIET: The bricks by the garage.
HILDA: I'll take care of them. What about Pauline?
JULIET: She won't betray me.
HILDA: You mustn't see her.
JULIET: But I—
HILDA: If you don't cut yourself off now you'll be dragged down with her.
JULIET: We promised each other we'd stay together no matter what.
HILDA: Don't be a stupid schoolgirl.
JULIET: We took a sacred oath.
HILDA: For Christ's sake!
JULIET: We have it all worked out. They'll put us in a mental institution for a year or two, then we'll be free to do as we like. It's rather a drastic solution I admit, but we were desperate.

Mrs Rieper was impossible. She didn't want to let go of Gina. But Gina has so much talent. She could be famous if—
HILDA: Will you shut up?
JULIET: But Mummy—
HILDA: If you want to survive you must give her up.
JULIET: I don't think I can.
HILDA, *looking hard into* JULIET's *eyes*: Give her up.

Scene Four

A prison cell. The same night.

A POLICE MATRON *is present. Pauline picks up a scrap of paper and begins writing.*

PAULINE: Tonight I find myself in a very unexpected place. The moider has been committed. The Hulmes have been wonderfully kind and sympathetic. Anyone would think I've been good. I've had a pleasant time with the police talking nineteen to the dozen and behaving as though I hadn't a care in the world. I have had no chance to talk to Deborah but am taking the blame for everything.

The MATRON *walks over to* PAULINE.

MATRON: Give it here, that's a good girl.
PAULINE: It's only a letter.
MATRON: Anything you write now can be used as evidence against you.
PAULINE: But it's private!
MATRON: Nothing's private any more. Hand it over. Come on.
PAULINE: No.

The MATRON *grabs* PAULINE, *twists her arm and forces her to drop the paper.*

Ah!
MATRON: I'm warning you. You'll find it much easier if you cooperate. *She goes out.*
PAULINE: No! Deborah? Deborah? I've been a stupid girl Deborah. A very, very stupid girl. I didn't realise...every word now is fatal.

> JULIET *is in her bedroom. She 'hears'* PAULINE *and makes up her mind to confess.*

JULIET: Blood has been shed to uphold our sacred vow. Together unto eternity.

⭐ Scene Five

The Hulmes' lounge. The next morning.

JULIET *is giving her statement to the* POLICE DETECTIVE. HILDA, PERRY *and* HENRY *are listening.*

JULIET: I, Juliet Hulme, saw Pauline Rieper hit her mother with the brick in the stocking. I took the stocking and hit her too. I thought one of them was going to die. I wanted to help Pauline. We both held her. After the first blow was struck I knew it would be necessary for us to kill her. The brick came out of the stocking with the force of the blows. *Pause.* May I see Gina now?

DETECTIVE: I'm sorry, no.

JULIET: Later on then?

DETECTIVE: We'll see. Get your things together.

> HILDA *stifles her tears.*

DETECTIVE: I'm sorry, Mrs Hulme.

JULIET, *kissing her mother*: Cheer up Mummy. I won't be long. Goodbye, Daddy.

HENRY: Do as you're told, Juliet.

JULIET: You too. 'Bye, Mr Perry. Look after Mummy for me. *To the* DETECTIVE: Shall we go?

> *She goes out with the* DETECTIVE.

HILDA: What do we do now?

HENRY: Come with me back to England. We can start over again.

HILDA: You're a fool, Henry. There's no going back now—for any of us.

> HENRY *goes out.* HILDA *stays with* PERRY.

✦ Scene Six

BRIDGET: The girls were charged with murder in the Christchurch Magistrates' Court on July 16th. There was a queue halfway down Armagh Street and I very nearly didn't get in.

   The High Court trial before Justice Adams was set for the 23rd of August. I made sure I was first in the queue for the public gallery this time. There was no way I was going to miss out.

   There was no question the girls had committed the murder. They'd both confessed almost straight away so the trial was only to say whether or not Pauline and Juliet were insane. The Defence had to prove they were. But how can you prove a body's insane if he's not sitting there, gibbering and foaming at the mouth? By hiring a fancy psychiatrist, that's how. One who's read so many books and done so much 'research' he's forgotten what 'good' and 'bad' mean. His name was Medlicott. Dr Reginald Medlicott.

An interview room in Paparua Prison.

MEDLICOTT: It's important you are very clear about this point, Juliet.

JULIET: I would be an absolute moron not to know murder was against the law. I don't believe we've done anything wrong. I know we've broken the law but morally we are without fault.

MEDLICOTT: So you consider yourself above the law?

JULIET: Of course. Gina and I have special insights that common people will never have. We have our own religion. We're writing our own Bible.

MEDLICOTT: You still worship a god?

JULIET: Oh yes. But not the Christian God. We worship god within ourselves. We have an extra part to our brains which lets us perceive beyond this world into Paradise. Only twenty-five people will be granted entry into the Fourth World.

MEDLICOTT: So this 'Fourth World' that you speak of is a real, physical place?

JULIET: We saw it at Port Levy. It's metaphorical in the sense that it's not exact but it's definitely there.

MEDLICOTT: Couldn't this world be part of your imagination?

JULIET: I know it's real.
PAULINE, *calling from far away*: Deborah! Deborah!

> *The sound of the sea.* PAULINE *appears out of the mist. The girls stand together, transfixed, on the edge of a cliff, looking out over Port Levy. Music and light surround them.*

JULIET: Gina! Look there! Shadows of angels on the waves. Twenty-three celestial beings. *She touches* PAULINE. Twenty-four.
PAULINE, *touching* JULIET: Twenty-five.
JULIET: As the prophets foretold, the doors of the Fourth World shall open for us and we shall join their exalted ranks.
PAULINE: Blessed be the saints, for they hold the key.
JULIET: The key to radiant life and truth everlasting.
PAULINE: Amen.
JULIET: Amen.

> PAULINE *disappears in the mist.*

MEDLICOTT: Other people might see this vision as part of a delusion.
JULIET: They don't matter. Gina matters. I matter. That's all. We have the right to do what we needed to do in the interests of our own happiness.

Another interview room, a day later.

MEDLICOTT: Hello, Pauline. How are you today?
PAULINE: I don't feel like talking.
MEDLICOTT: Why not?
PAULINE: Because you are an irritating fool, displeasing to look at, and have an irritating way of speaking.
MEDLICOTT: I'm here to help you. And in order to do that we need to talk.
PAULINE: 'A' for effort. I have a headache.
MEDLICOTT: Do you get them often?
PAULINE: Yes. I see things.
MEDLICOTT: Can you describe them to me?
PAULINE, *making it up as she goes along*: They're visions of hellish flames and blinding light. Sometimes I feel this terrible impulse to thrust my hand into the fire and watch it burn.
MEDLICOTT: Oh? Do you?

ACT II

PAULINE: I think I could be ill.
MEDLICOTT: You're concerned about your state of health?
PAULINE: Ill in my mind, not my body, you idiot.
MEDLICOTT: How have you been sleeping?
PAULINE: Not well.
MEDLICOTT: Oh?
PAULINE: Is 'Oh' the only word you know?
MEDLICOTT: Why didn't you sleep well last night?
PAULINE: I forgot and fell asleep on my right side. If I sleep on the right I dream about Mother . . . only that I hurt her and haven't killed her. She comes back and she's rather nice. You wouldn't be able to get me a photo of Mario Lanza would you? Or James Mason?
MEDLICOTT: Tell me about your mother.
PAULINE: My mother was holding me back. That's all I'm going to say.
MEDLICOTT: What do you want the photos for?
PAULINE: To keep me company. They're saints.
MEDLICOTT: Yesterday you said you went through the saints together with Juliet.
PAULINE: Each of the saints has his own personality . . . his own way of doing things . . . things like . . . making love. It's very amusing. We become the saints. Do I have to spell it out?
MEDLICOTT: Not unless you want to.
PAULINE: Are you in the habit of lying?
MEDLICOTT: No. I'm not.
PAULINE: Deborah said you'll make certain we're together.
MEDLICOTT: That's a misunderstanding.
PAULINE: She said you'd take care of it.
MEDLICOTT: What happens to you both after the trial isn't up to me. I can only make recommendations.
PAULINE: What would you recommend?
MEDLICOTT: Some time apart would probably be beneficial.
PAULINE: I hope New Zealand is bombed and you're directly underneath!
MEDLICOTT: Why do you say that?
PAULINE: What a witless cretin you are, Dr Medlicott. How did you ever become a psychiatrist?

Scene Seven

BRIDGET: The trial went on six days. Everybody and his dog testified—but not Juliet or Pauline. They sat there, at the heart of the murder, silent as two stones. Their own lawyers wouldn't let them talk because they were too clever—if you heard them talking you'd know they weren't crazy. See? Simple logic.

I'll tell you what got up my nose. The court in its wisdom decided that Dr Hulme was too important to be bothered with trivial matters like murder. He'd snuck off to England well before the trial. But they dragged Mr Rieper into the box—him with his wife bashed by his own daughter. Now that's British justice for you.

The courtroom.

BROWN *questions* MR RIEPER.

BROWN: Mr Rieper. Would you say Pauline was a normal little girl?
MR RIEPER: Yes. Except for having osteomy—osteomylitis.
BROWN: These operations caused Pauline considerable pain?
MR RIEPER: Yes, they did.
BROWN: And the doctor advised that she should not play games in case she might damage her limbs?
MR RIEPER: No violent games. But she did modelling in Plasticine and wood and was fairly good at it.
BROWN: How were your relations with Pauline up until the time she met Juliet?
MR RIEPER: We were very good friends.
BROWN: And with her mother?
MR RIEPER: They were the same.
BROWN: Did you ever see any signs that your daughter was abnormal in any way?
BRIDGET: I saw them kissing once. In bed. I should have said something.
MR RIEPER: Juliet seemed to be her chief interest in life.
BROWN: Her friendship with Juliet was very intense?
BRIDGET: They were queer.
MR RIEPER: She cut her mother and me out of her affections.

BRIDGET: There. I've finally said it.
BROWN: Pauline had a great many records?
MR RIEPER: Yes. Opera and that sort of thing.
BROWN: She was interested in clothes?
MR RIEPER: After she met Juliet, yes.
BROWN: She had a horse?
MR RIEPER: Yes.
BROWN: And a boyfriend?
MR RIEPER: She was friendly with a boy who stayed with us last year for a short time. He was one of our boarders.
BROWN: Records, clothes, horses, boys, a crush on a girlfriend from a glamorous family. Would you not say these were typical adolescent preoccupations?
MR RIEPER: I suppose so.
BROWN: Before this, did you ever feel there was ever any need for medical attention to Pauline as far as her brain was concerned?
MR RIEPER: She treated me with disdain and all that, but apart from that—no.
BROWN: Thank you, Mr Rieper.

    MR RIEPER *goes out.*

BRIDGET: Pauline Rieper, the fishmonger's daughter . . . did she show any remorse at her poor father's testimony? Not a flicker. The trial was a picnic to those girls. They came and went each day from Paparua Prison, like they didn't have a care in the world. You'd have thought they were having a holiday at the seaside.

Scene Eight

Paparua Prison. A dining room.

The girls are eating their pudding. The MATRON *is present.*

JULIET: You think Mr Gresson looks like James Mason?
PAULINE: He has the same eyes. Big soft eyes.
JULIET: Like a deer. Like Bambi.
PAULINE: Bambi Gresson!

MATRON: Eat your pudding.
JULIET: We are. *To* PAULINE: Have you noticed Mummy? She looks terrible. She'd better watch out or Signor Perry might lose interest.
PAULINE: She looks sad.
JULIET: Why should she be sad?
PAULINE: She'll miss you.
JULIET: Don't be stupid. She doesn't miss Daddy. She doesn't miss my brother. Why should she miss me?
PAULINE: If you could choose any prison which one would it be?
JULIET: Mt Eden sounds rather fascinating. Pseudo-medieval. We could write the second instalment of the Adventures of Lancelot Trelawny there.
PAULINE: I dreamed about it last night.
JULIET: I told you. Lie on your left side, then you won't.
PAULINE: Most of the dream was about my father though. He was chopping off a fish-head.
JULIET: Don't talk about your family. It depresses me.
PAULINE: Sorry.
JULIET: This is only temporary. A passing phenomenon. Live outside of it.

JULIET caresses PAULINE.

Don't be weak. We can't be weak.
MATRON, *looking up*: That's enough of that. Have you two finished your pudding?
JULIET: Yes, thank you.
MATRON: Seconds?
PAULINE: Oh no. We have an abomination for mush.

The girls snicker.

MATRON: Laugh now, go on. You won't be laughing once you're in prison.
JULIET: We can always find ways to keep ourselves amused.
MATRON: You're not such a fool as to think you'll still be together?
JULIET: I've spoken to Mr Gresson and Dr Medlicott and it's all arranged.
MATRON: They never put lesbians together. Regulations.
JULIET: We're a special case.

MATRON: Tell that to the Judge. He'd love to hang you both.
JULIET: We're under age.
MATRON: Lucky for you. He's is a mean-minded teetotal Baptist shit and you won't find any ounce of sympathy from him—or any of the jury.
JULIET: We weren't expecting sympathy. Not from this world.
MATRON: Three more days.
PAULINE: Leave us alone.
MATRON: Then we'll see who's laughing.
BRIDGET: They carried on like characters in some larger than life-sized novel of theirs, while Hilda Hulme aged by the hour.

    HILDA HULME *enters.*

Lo, how the mighty are fallen.

Scene Nine

GRESSON'*s chambers. Early evening.*

GRESSON: What can I do for you, Mrs Hulme?
HILDA: Win this case, Mr Gresson.
GRESSON: I'm doing the best I can.
HILDA: It's not good enough. Alan Brown is already pouring the champagne. He ripped shreds off you today in court.
GRESSON: The defence hasn't presented its case yet.
HILDA: Juliet is fifteen and a half. She's an extraordinarily gifted child who's been led astray.
GRESSON: Unfortunately the facts don't quite lend themselves to that interpretation.
HILDA: For God's sake. She's ill. She needs help.
GRESSON: This is exactly the point we'll be making tomorrow. Reg Medlicott has put together a very strong argument.
HILDA: Henry hasn't sent me any money since he left. If it weren't for Mr Perry I'd be eating the bark off trees.
GRESSON: You must be tired.
HILDA: There's something else.
GRESSON: You do realise this conference is highly irregular.
HILDA: I do.
GRESSON: Well?

HILDA: I object to the way the word homosexual is being bandied about, Mr Gresson. Surely that label serves no useful purpose.
GRESSON: The label tells us something.
HILDA: Something ugly and unnecessary.
GRESSON: Mrs Hulme, you must appreciate my position. I have to convince the jury Juliet and Pauline are insane. Homosexuality is recognised as a diagnostic indication of insanity by the psychiatric profession.
HILDA: Surely mental illness defies these kinds of repulsive pigeon holes.
GRESSON: Legally speaking I'm tied, Mrs Hulme. We must prove, beyond a shadow of a doubt, that the accused did not know the nature and quality of their act. Whatever labels I have to use I will, to show the girls are—and were—deluded and living in a state of unreality.
HILDA: My daughter is not a lesbian.
GRESSON: You can rest assured I've formed no personal judgement, Mrs Hulme.
HILDA: You can win the case without sensationalising their friendship, surely.
GRESSON: This really is Dr Medlicott's territory—
HILDA: Their relationship obviously was unhealthy—but there was nothing sexual about it.
GRESSON: Pauline's diaries suggest that—
HILDA: Her diaries are largely works of fiction, Mr Gresson. I thought we'd been through that.
GRESSON: Yes, of course.
HILDA: Thank you. I'm sorry if I've been overstepping my mark. It's been a very trying time.
GRESSON: I appreciate that.
HILDA: This is a backward country, Mr Gresson. Being Cambridge educated yourself, I'm sure you will understand. There are twelve simple men sitting on that jury. Our only hope is to make them feel pity.
GRESSON: Pity, yes.
HILDA: I've thought about it for quite some time. Those twelve simple men may possibly be able to feel pity for two schoolgirls—but they will never find it in their hearts to feel pity for two homosexuals.

GRESSON: No?
HILDA: No, Mr Gresson. Thank you. *She goes out.*

Scene Ten

BRIDGET: By now the courtroom was swimming with contradictions and useless talk. Dr Medlicott insisted Pauline and Juliet were certifiable and the Crown doctors said just the opposite. He said, she said, he said—on and on it went... and were we any closer to the truth? Not in my book.

The courtroom.

BROWN *is cross-examining* MEDLICOTT.

BROWN: Dr Medlicott, are the accused insane from a legal point of view?
MEDLICOTT: To my mind, they are.
BROWN: During your interviews they tried to impress upon you they were insane?
MEDLICOTT: On several occasions, yes.
BROWN: Why would they want to be held insane?
MEDLICOTT: I don't know clearly.
BROWN: Have you formed any theory?
MEDLICOTT: I think it quite possible they thought being insane might lessen the time of their detention.
BROWN: But the girls knew the penalty before they killed Mrs Rieper?
MEDLICOTT: At my first interview with Parker on June 27 she said she knew murder was considered wrong.
BROWN: Well, that is one admission anyway.
GRESSON: That is comment, Your Honour, and my friend knows quite well he should refrain from comment while evidence is being given.
BROWN: I am sorry, Your Honour. I should not have made it. Dr Medlicott, adolescence is a difficult period, isn't it?
MEDLICOTT: Yes.
BROWN: I take it you were an adolescent once?
MEDLICOTT: I think we can all agree on that.

BROWN: Did you have a difficult period, Dr Medlicott?
MEDLICOTT: I refuse to answer that question about myself.
BROWN: You referred to adolescent 'pashes'?
MEDLICOTT: Yes. The girl wants to do the type of things the person she is fond of does.
BROWN: Yet you say there was no proof of any physical relationship?
MEDLICOTT: Absolutely none. Homosexuality means love between persons of the same sex which may be platonic only.
BROWN: To ordinary persons like myself homosexuality is taken to mean a physical relationship between persons of the same sex.
MEDLICOTT: Well that is a completely erroneous point of view. I know many people who are homosexual and they have no physical relationship at all.
BROWN: Your reading of the diaries showed these young people played about with each other sexually?
MEDLICOTT: It is very suggestive but there is no clear evidence of it.
BROWN: There is also very plain evidence so far as Parker is concerned that she had sexual intercourse with a boy?
MEDLICOTT: There is no evidence she got any erotic involvement out of it.
BROWN: But she did have intercourse with the boy over and over again?
MEDLICOTT: No, only once.
BROWN: Over and over again?
MEDLICOTT: No, only once.
BROWN: I stand corrected. I've misread my notes. But she attempted to have it more than once?
MEDLICOTT: It would appear so.
BROWN: You placed a considerable importance on the girls' cool demeanour after they got over the sudden shock of the killing.
MEDLICOTT: I think it is an aspect of their condition.
BROWN: Was not Judas Iscariot cool and calm when he took bread and wine with our Lord?
ADAMS: Mr Brown. Whatever the temptation I think it would be advisable not to continue that topic.
MEDLICOTT: A pity, as it would lead us to Judas hanging himself.
BROWN: Let us take other figures of history, doctor. Did not Macbeth murder Duncan at the instigation of Lady Macbeth?

Act II

MEDLICOTT: Yes.
BROWN: Was she mad?
MEDLICOTT: No.
BROWN: Did she not act before and after the murder exactly as these girls did?
MEDLICOTT: No. These girls have no contrition. Lady Macbeth was stricken with remorse.
GRESSON: What is the medical question arising out of Lady Macbeth and her activities?
BROWN: I'm surprised Mr Gresson does not see the point of this.
GRESSON: I'd be surprised if anyone could.
BROWN: Dr Medlicott, this case deals with crime and insanity.
MEDLICOTT: It does.
BROWN: Have you ever heard of two insane people combining to commit a crime?
MEDLICOTT: It is quite within the possibilities of the folie à deux paranoia to join in and plan the committing of a crime.
BROWN: You believe they are grossly insane and certifiable?
MEDLICOTT: Absolutely.
BROWN: Does it not disconcert you that three experienced psychiatrists disagree with you?
MEDLICOTT: I would say there was an unfortunate difference of medical opinion. It does not alter my opinion.
BROWN: Did these two young persons, when they attacked Mrs Rieper, know what they were doing?
MEDLICOTT: They knew what they were doing.
BROWN: Did they know the nature and quality of their act?
MEDLICOTT: They did.
BROWN: Did they know they were wrong according to the law?
MEDLICOTT: They did, but they did not recognise the law.
BRIDGET: But the law is the law. Like God is God. You can't remake the universe to suit yourself. The universe is, and you fit into it. Isn't that so? When Mr Gresson summed up he tried to tell us ordinary folk we weren't fit to judge these matters.
GRESSON, *addressing the jury*: The diagnosis of the exact nature of a mental illness is a matter for competent psychiatrists or doctors and is not one for the layman to decide. Dr Medlicott told you in his considered opinion the two accused suffer

from a paranoia of the exalted type in a setting of folie à deux. In other words the two accused are insane.

BRIDGET: They can't be. Didn't Dr Medlicott say they knew what they were doing?

GRESSON: Dr Medlicott gave you grounds for this statement. The girls had their own religion, they were gods, they were outstanding geniuses, they showed an intense and gross homosexuality. They even set out to break all the Ten Commandments; they have committed blackmail, theft, cheating and murder. Some of you will have—as I have—daughters of your own. Suppose one of them showed even half these symptoms. Do you mean to tell me you would not get the doctor in to her? Isn't it plain, and wouldn't anybody say, if the facts were proved about a girl, she is—in common language—crackers?

BRIDGET: No, Mr Gresson. You're sadly misguided.

GRESSON: These are mentally ill adolescents whom competent medical opinion has considered insane. They are not brutal criminals; at the time they committed the crime they were ill and not criminally responsible for their actions.

BRIDGET: I looked into their faces—Pauline and Juliet—and I saw them as they were. Two precocious dirty-minded little girls.

GRESSON: I now conclude my case for the defence.

BRIDGET: Two pathetic girls with grand ideas of something more. Two empty vessels waiting to be filled. *Pause.* It only took the jury two hours to make their decision.

ADAMS: Pauline Yvonne Parker—guilty. Juliet Marion Hulme—guilty. Have either of the prisoners anything to say?

GRESSON: No, Your Honour.

ADAMS: The sentence of the court is detention during Her Majesty's pleasure. The prisoners may now be removed.

The court clears. The MATRON *leads the girls away.*

Act ii

⭐ Scene Eleven

A holding cell in the court building.

The MATRON *guards* JULIET *and* PAULINE.

JULIET: Hello, Bambi.
GRESSON: I'm terribly sorry, Juliet. I feel I've failed you.
JULIET: Is it true that wig on your head is made of horsehair? Gina and I have a bet on it. Is it?
GRESSON: Yes. It is.
JULIET, *mouthing to* PAULINE: I told you so.
GRESSON: Your mother would like to see you now. She asked me especially to arrange a meeting.
JULIET: Bambi, you're going to miss your rugby game in Lancaster Park with all this idle chat.
GRESSON: She's terribly upset about the verdict.
JULIET: My mother can see me with Gina or not at all.
GRESSON: Try to imagine how she feels.
JULIET: I'm insane. Remember?
GRESSON: You may not get the chance later on. Please. For her sake.
JULIET: Have I ever told you how foolish you look in that get up?
GRESSON: Many times. I'm worried about you, Juliet. We all are.
JULIET: That's jolly decent of you.
GRESSON: You don't seem to realise that you need help.
JULIET: You too. I think you're a very melancholy man. Why don't you treat yourself to a holiday?
GRESSON: Listen to me. This is no time for schoolgirl games.
JULIET: Gina and I are counting on your recommendation to the Minister.
GRESSON: You must accept your situation.
JULIET: You botched the case, Bambi. It's the least you could do.
GRESSON: There's help and support if you'll only take it.
JULIET: You're an odd fish but I like you, Bambi. I always have. Better luck next time.

> GRESSON *gives up. He leaves* JULIET *and* PAULINE *and meets up with* HILDA *and* PERRY.

PERRY: Mr Gresson?

GRESSON: Mr Perry.

> *They shake hands.*

PERRY: We appreciate everything you've done.
GRESSON: I'm terribly sorry, Mrs Hulme. I did everything I could but—
HILDA: She's only fifteen. She thinks it's a game. She—*She breaks down.*
PERRY: Darling, don't.
HILDA: They were baying for blood. Brown, and that pig, Adams. As if there hadn't been enough blood already.
GRESSON: Please accept my sympathy.
HILDA: You're sorry. I'm sorry. Everyone's sorry. Everyone but Juliet. Where is she?
GRESSON: She's in the holding cell.
HILDA: May I see her? Alone?
GRESSON: She still insists on Pauline being there.
HILDA: It's like a disease . . . take me home, Walter.

> PERRY *takes* HILDA*'s arm.*

One more thing, Mr Gresson.
GRESSON: Yes?
HILDA: Whatever it takes . . . separate them.

✧ Scene Twelve

A room in Paparua Prison.

The girls have their coats on and suitcases beside them. PAULINE *has a notebook.*

PAULINE. *reading:* '. . . "Roland," said Carmelita tenderly. "Your life is a tragedy . . ."'
JULIET: Concentrate.
PAULINE: '"How can I stay with you now that you've shot Roderick?" Suddenly Vendetta reared on his hind legs—'
JULIET: 'Powerful hind legs' would be better.
PAULINE: '—powerful hind legs, pawing the air and snorting . . .' What if what Matron said is true?

ACT II

JULIET: Will you stop worrying? Matron is a minion. Read.
PAULINE: No, you.
JULIET: 'Vendetta crashed down on Carmelita. She fell sideways to the ground. Roland knelt over her. "Darling," he sobbed. Vendetta answered with a wild scream. He galloped into the sunset. His revenge was complete.'

Silence.

When the car comes you simply climb in beside me.
PAULINE: She said there was a letter from the Minister of Justice.
JULIET: Bambi told me personally it was all arranged.
PAULINE: When?
JULIET: We come as a pair. Like the King and Queen of Hearts. Why would they want to split us up?
PAULINE: They did before the trial.
JULIET: For a few days' psychiatric assessment. That's all. Did I tell you I have a new Latin lover?
PAULINE: Cicero. Yes.
JULIET: Laugh, darling. If you can't laugh they've won.

PAULINE *embraces* JULIET

PAULINE: You're very, very special to me, Deborah.
JULIET: And you're my Gina. Always.
PAULINE: Promise?
JULIET: Cross my heart.
PAULINE: And hope to die.

The MATRON *and a* PRISON OFFICER *enter.*

MATRON: Break it up, girls. The car's here. Not you, Parker.
JULIET: There's obviously been some mix-up. We were told—
MATRON: You were told, Hulme to Mt Eden today, Parker to Arohata Borstal next week.
JULIET: I insist on speaking with the Superintendent.
MATRON: I'm in charge here.
PAULINE: Deborah?
MATRON: It's like the army. You get your marching orders and you march.
OFFICER: Do as Matron says—let's not have any trouble.
PAULINE: Deborah!

JULIET: No! Stay away from me! I won't go unless Gina comes too!
MATRON: We'll carry you out to the car if we have to. Now be reasonable.
PAULINE: Look out!

The OFFICER *pins* JULIET*'s arms behind her back.*

JULIET: Let go of me, you disgusting bastard! Gina! Help me!
MATRON: Don't you move, Parker.
OFFICER: Out to the car. Come on, there's a good girl.
JULIET: Get away from me! No! You can't do this! No! Gina! Help me!

JULIET *screams and struggles as she is carried off. A car door slams.* PAULINE *stands completely still as the car drives away.*

MATRON: It's much better if you cooperate. Are you going to cooperate?

Silence.

I think you should. Come on. Pick up your suitcase.

PAULINE *slowly picks it up.*

Back to your room. Good.

Scene Thirteen

BRIDGET: The authorities sent Juliet to Auckland and Pauline to Wellington. Prise them apart and reform them, that was the idea. No communication, plain food and lessons by correspondence. If you can't reform clever girls with hard work and education, who can you reform?

Five years passed. Hilda and lover-boy were overseas somewhere, living the high life no doubt. Dr Hulme was making nuclear bombs at Aldermaston. Old Mr Rieper was carrying on in Christchurch as best he could. And me? I was biding my time, waiting to see what God required of me. When I heard Pauline had embraced the Faith, and was back in Christchurch in preparation for her release, I took it as a sign.

PAULINE *and* JULIET *are in their separate cells.*

The MATRON *leads* BRIDGET *to* PAULINE'*s cell.*

PAULINE: Mrs O'Malley.
BRIDGET: Hello, Pauline.
PAULINE: What a surprise.
BRIDGET: Thought I'd forgotten you, eh?
PAULINE: No.
BRIDGET: What's all these books then?
PAULINE: I'm studying for my degree.
BRIDGET, *picking up a book*: Coming of Age in Samoa . . . my, my, a regular little professor . . .
JULIET: My dear Gina. I'm speaking to you through the spirits of the Fourth World and trust you hear me per usual. They finally set my release date—the 16th of November 1959. I had rather hoped for the 28th of October—my glorious twentieth birthday—but nobody in this dump has any sense of occasion.

Have I mentioned to you Mummy's letter-writing campaign? It's growing more and more fervent. Every paragraph praises bucolic England and urges me to forget this dreary little colony with all its attendant memories. Starting over is her theme song as if all I am now must be erased. The girl without a past. I'm to change my name by deed poll, devise a fictitious history and step, newly minted, onto England's happy shore.
BRIDGET: Pauline, I'm still talking to you.
PAULINE: What is it you want?
BRIDGET: I heard the good news.
PAULINE: Oh? What good news is that?
BRIDGET: That you've embraced the faith! God's mercy is limitless; vast as the ocean, deep as the sea.
JULIET: I've heard a rather disturbing rumour recently. Some screw told me you've become a Catholic. I hope most passionately it isn't true. It would indicate a serious character defect on your part. What could you possibly want from the Virgin Mary?
BRIDGET: You still think about her, don't you?
PAULINE: Mother? No. Not much.

BRIDGET: I was referring to Juliet Hulme.
JULIET: Do you know the first thing I'm going to do when I get out? I'm going to climb to the top of a hill and embrace the sky. Not just a mingy strip of sky, but all of it, unfettered and stretching to eternity. Then I'll roll in the grass—the grass that is just beginning to smell of summer and sun—and I'll press myself flat against the earth and pay homage. And when I finish crying—for I'm certain I will cry at long, long last—I'll shut my eyes, surrender myself to the universe—and wait for you.
BRIDGET: Will you pray with me Pauline? I came here so we could pray together. *She prays.* 'Oh my God, I am heartily sorry'—don't resist it girl.

PAULINE *joins in. The sound of the sea at Port Levy competes.*

BRIDGET *and* PAULINE *together*: I am heartily sorry for having offended thee and I detest sin above every other evil because it offends thee my God who art worthy of all my love and I firmly resolve, by thy holy Grace, never more to offend thee and to amend my life. Amen.
PAULINE: Bridget. I wondered if—?
BRIDGET: The answer is no.
PAULINE: As a favour.
BRIDGET: Are you daft? Why should I risk my neck to help the two of you?
PAULINE: Please. I wouldn't dare ask if I didn't think it was God's will.
BRIDGET: God's will! Now that's bold.
PAULINE: She's getting out two weeks before me. They've done it deliberately.
BRIDGET: The whole world will be watching you.
PAULINE: I'm begging you, Bridget. Tell Juliet to wait for me.
BRIDGET: Maybe she wants to forget you. Ever thought of that?
PAULINE: We made a vow.
BRIDGET: You can't take up where you left off or you'll both end up in Hell, mark my words.
PAULINE: Perhaps we're already there.
BRIDGET: You're still in the grip, girl. Just like I thought.

ACT II

PAULINE: Help me, Bridget.
BRIDGET: The eyes of God are on us both, Pauline.
PAULINE: I know that.
BRIDGET: All right then. I'll do what has to be done.

JULIET's *cell, a few days later.* BRIDGET *enters.*

JULIET: Bridget O'Malley! To what may we attribute this unexpected pleasure?
BRIDGET: Hello, Juliet. It's been a long time.
JULIET: Why are you here?
BRIDGET: I brought you some biscuits.
JULIET: All this way—and all this time—for a bag of biscuits?
BRIDGET: I've just seen Pauline. She asked me to get a message to you.
JULIET: I knew it. I knew Gina wouldn't fail me.
BRIDGET: Is it safe to talk?
JULIET: Yes. But quickly.
BRIDGET: Pauline told me to tell you she's getting out on the 29th.
JULIET: I know that. Everybody knows that.
BRIDGET: You're not to wait for her.
JULIET: What?
BRIDGET: She remembers your vow but she considers it no longer binding in the light of all that's happened.
JULIET: Liar.
BRIDGET: Why would I come all the way from Christchurch on the bus and the train and the ferry to tell you a lie? Pauline has found God's infinite mercy. She's changed her name. She's making a complete break with the past.
JULIET: No!
BRIDGET: Pauline's not the same person you knew five years ago. That Pauline has vanished. Don't try and find her.
JULIET: I will not be broken.
BRIDGET: Leave her Juliet. It's finished.
JULIET: Thank you Bridget. You can go now.
BRIDGET: I'm sure she'd like to know you wished her well.
JULIET: Get out of here.
BRIDGET: I suppose you'll be looking forward to seeing your mother. She's Mrs Perry now I hear.
JULIET: I said get out.

BRIDGET: I'll be praying for you Juliet. Remember God's arms are open to all sinners.
JULIET: GET OUT!

PAULINE's *cell, a week later.*

PAULINE: You saw her?
BRIDGET: I saw her.
PAULINE: How did she look? Was she the same?
BRIDGET: She was her usual self. Prison suits her.
PAULINE: Tell me exactly what she said.
BRIDGET: Gina.
PAULINE: She still calls me Gina?
BRIDGET: That's right.
PAULINE: Go slowly. I want to savour it.
BRIDGET: Gina. You must not expect me to wait for you. Our vow no longer binds us. Everything is finished. Do not try to find me.
PAULINE: You're lying.
BRIDGET: I don't need to lie.
PAULINE: You're leaving something out then.
BRIDGET: No. It's word for word. 'Our vow no longer binds us.' Now you can walk out and start over again. Don't you see? You're truly free at last. There's a new life waiting out there for you.
PAULINE: No!
BRIDGET: It's what she said.
PAULINE: Are you telling me the truth?
BRIDGET: Yes. It's God's truth, Pauline. God's truth.

BRIDGET *leaves.* PAULINE *weeps. Then she hears* JULIET's *voice. With it comes radiant light, music and the eternal sea.*

JULIET: I want you to remember Paradise. It was ours once. We created our own map of Heaven. Now that I have been brought to my knees I see our star brighter than ever. I will never give in.
PAULINE: I will never look back.
JULIET: I will never regret.
PAULINE: It is our fate.

BOTH: I worship the power of these lovely two
With that adoring love known to so few.
'Tis indeed a miracle one must feel
That two such heavenly creatures are real.